Finally discover your worth and be transformed from the inside out!

THE *Brave* BODY METHOD

HOW TO WIN THE WAR ON WEIGHT
& GAIN SELF-ACCEPTANCE IN 4 EASY STEPS

emerge
publishing

TULSA, OKLAHOMA

19 18 17 16   10 9 8 7 6 5 4 3 2 1

THE BRAVE BODY METHOD
How to Win the War on Weight & Gain Self-Acceptance in 4 Easy Steps

www.eileenwilder.com

All Scripture quotations, unless otherwise indicated, are taken from the Amplified Bible, Copyright © 1954, 1958, 1962, 1964, 1965, 1987 by The Lockman Foundation. Used by permission.

Published by:
Emerge Publishing, LLC
9521B Riverside Parkway, Suite 243
Tulsa, Oklahoma 74137
888.407.4447
www.EmergePublishing.com

emerge
p u b l i s h i n g
TULSA, OKLAHOMA

Cover Design: Christian Ophus | Emerge Publishing, LLC
Interior Design: Anita Stumbo

Library of Congress Cataloging-in-Publication Data

BISAC Category: HEA019000 HEALTH & FITNESS / Diet & Nutrition / Weight Loss and SEL023000 SELF-HELP / Personal Growth / Self-Esteem

Other Formats: Kindle / Nook / iBook
Hardcover ISBN: 978-1-943127-20-7
E-book ISBN: 978-1-943127-21-4

Printed in the United States of America

What People Are Saying

My Struggles Are Finally Over   ★ ★ ★ ★ ★
I am happy to say that it truly feels like my struggles are finally over. I recommend this book to anyone out there who is struggling with weight or self-esteem issues. —A.K.

Dragged My Laptop From Room To Room ...
Couldn't Stop Reading!   ★ ★ ★ ★ ★
I couldn't stop reading! I literally dragged my laptop from room to room with me as I prepared breakfast, got ready for the day and finally put everything else on hold so I could sit down and finish this book. I LOVED the scriptures and the idea of daily meditation. I mean ... I know this stuff, well, at least I thought I did! —J.C.

Not Just About Weight Loss   ★ ★ ★ ★ ★
This is NOT just a weight loss book. It's a book about truly seeing yourself through God's eyes and speaking power into your life and your self image. Eileen's scriptures are resonating and her prayers are powerful. Her openness and vulnerability made me feel so close and so connected to her. It's a fun and quick read, but one that I will keep at my fingertips so I can always refer back to it. A must-have read! —D.J.

I Giggled With Excitement   ★ ★ ★ ★ ★
I literally giggled with excitement when I read The Brave Body Method. *I think my soul jumped for joy! Eileen's method can be applied to not only achieving weight loss, but also to every other aspect of our lives. You should definitely read this and find out for yourself! I can't wait to share it with all of my sisters and girlfriends.* —E.K.

If You Are Tired Of The Yo-Yo Dieting And The Weight Cycling, This Book Is For You ... ★ ★ ★ ★ ★
In The Brave Body Method, *the author Eileen Wilder shares candidly about her struggles with her weight, eating disorders, self-esteem and anxiety. Based on biblical principles, Eileen lays out the steps she took to overcome them and shows you how you can do it too. These steps cannot only be applied to win the battle on weight but to every area of our lives. After reading this book, I find myself feeling empowered to care for my body in a new way ... from the inside out! —L.F.*

Shook Something Loose In My Spirit ★ ★ ★ ★ ★
The Brave Body Method *literally shook something loose in my spirit when reading it ... a revelation, an awakening! I read Eileen's book at a time when I was seriously suffering from internal devil-dialog ... just the negative self-talk that holds women back from seeing ourselves the way God intends us to—as masterpieces! I was so convinced that I had done something to displease God ... that I wanted to place blame and fault on myself ... that I had lost the understanding of the meaning and relevance of God's grace. Reading Eileen's book was a slap that I needed, in the best sort of way! —D.J.*

I Was Positive For Others, Never For Myself ★ ★ ★ ★ ★
This book is exactly what women need who are struggling like I was with low self-esteem and self-confidence. I used to focus on the positive in others ... but couldn't do that for myself. After implementing The Brave Body Method, *I am speaking positive thoughts and Scriptures and I feel incredible! —S.B.*

I Tried Everything Else, Until Now   ★ ★ ★ ★ ★
Before reading The Brave Body Method, *I had tried everything to get my health and the way I thought about myself "right." After reading and implementing* The Brave Body Method, *I realized I was missing a key component ... God! I had invited him to every area of my life but not THIS! Once I did that everything changed. And I have this book to thank for it. It has totally changed my life and the way I view myself! —M.H.*

Now God Is In Control, Not Me   ★ ★ ★ ★ ★
I am dedicated to fitness training and I do not suffer from weight issues, but as I came to the end of the book, I realized I had never invited God into this part of my life. I am excited to see how improved these areas in my life can be with GOD in control, not me. —C.K.

Now I KNOW God Is With Me   ★ ★ ★ ★ ★
I used to struggle with feeling alone in my journey to lose weight, but since I started doing The Brave Body Method *I understand that God is with me. I will never be alone anymore, and I feel strong and have a purpose in this journey: to be as healthy as He wants me to be! —C.A.*

Simple And Practical   ★ ★ ★ ★ ★
This book is for anyone who struggles with weight. It's easy to read, and you will learn practical steps that will motivate you in your everyday life. Eileen gives you easy exercises, a daily action guide, it's simple and you will be encouraged. A great book to read! —S.S.

Quite Possibly The *Missing Link Between Losing Weight And Keeping It Off*   ★ ★ ★ ★ ★

This is NOT the latest fad diet nor is it a quick fix to loose 5 pounds in 5 days. The Brave Body Method is a holistic approach to weight loss. It promotes becoming healthy from the inside out, so you can lose the weight and keep it off. The Method helps you discover the root cause on the inside of you that is producing the undesirable results on the outside of you. The book pulls together interesting research, biblical principles, inspirational quotes, and the author's personal story of how she overcame an eating disorder using this method. —A.S.

Could Not Put It Down   ★ ★ ★ ★ ★

It can be hard to find a clear, actionable plan to move toward hope and change when it comes to how I see myself and what I think I should look like or should be—not only could I not put this book down, The Brave Body Method is filled with truth and easy-to-apply steps that lead to becoming healthier—mind and body. The author's stories are relatable and I'm already taking steps from this book toward being brave! Excited and hopeful for where this may lead—would recommend this method to anyone. —K.F.

Specific Instructions To Keep You Accountable   ★ ★ ★ ★ ★

The Brave Body Method *is a motivational book that refreshingly doesn't focus on a diet or exercise regimen. The Method explains, by embracing God's grace and truth, you can achieve health goals that have in the past seemed difficult and insurmountable. The content keeps you accountable to what you are doing by providing specific instructions on getting started. I enjoyed the book and recommend it to anyone is ready to try a new approach. —C.K.*

As we are liberated from our own fears,
Our presence automatically liberates others.
—NELSON MANDELA

CONTENTS

Foreword 11

Introduction: The Secret of The Method 15

STEP 1: "K"—KNOW YOU ARE HOT

1. Excuse Me, Your Behind Is in My Way. 27
2. You Are What You Think You Are 35
3. The 4:8 Filter 43
4. You Are a Masterpiece 49
5. You Are a God-Pod 55
6. You Are a Target. 61

STEP 2: "I"—INFLICT DAMAGE

7. Speak Only What You Seek 77
8. Develop a Brave Vocabulary. 89

STEP 3: "S"—SEE THE GOD-PAINTING

9. Vision Board for Your Soul. 101
10. The God-Painting Will Take Your Breath Away 109
11. How to See the God-Painting in 7 Easy Steps 121

STEP 4: "S"—START BEFORE YOU ARE READY

12. Act As If. 135
13. Resistance: The War Is Over Your Seed of Action 145
14. Three Seeds for Maximum Results 151

Brave Body Method 21-Day Plan. 161

Brave Body Method 21-Day Action Guide. 165

Bonus Chapter: Emotional Exhaustion 167

End Notes 185

About the Author. 189

Foreword

CHANGED

WHEN I FIRST MET EILEEN, she was a quiet, shy freshman in college. I was surprised, when one day after church, she approached me to mentor her. Gladly I said yes and began getting to know this eighteen-year-old, who I could see from the start, had a huge reservoir of untapped potential.

Over hot coffee, nestled in on my living room couch every week, we met with Bibles open and hearts ablaze as we unpacked the promises of God and practically applied them to her everyday life.

Amidst this warm, caffeine-infused conversation, something special began happening. The transforming power in God's Word started to change Eileen from the inside out. She was discovering her identity, and it was astounding to watch.

Her transformation was rapid and inspiring. She went from shy to bold, from insecure to a recognizable confidence. Ten years later, in 2008, my husband, Dennis and I, had the privilege of ordaining her as a pastor on our team. We not only married her and her husband but also had the joy of dedicating their three beautiful babies.

The inherent power in the Word never ceases to take my breath away.

Eileen's story is really our collective story—God taking the broken pieces of our lives and making us brave. In this book you will find the keys that made Eileen brave, and I am sure they will for you, too.

You see, I believe God has already written "brave" in the narrative of YOUR story.

Whether you will be reading *The Brave Body Method* over

a hot coffee or nestled into your favorite chair, my prayer is that you, too, experience the same lavish grace Eileen did so many years ago ... and ... be changed from the inside out.

Cheering you on,

DONNA PISANI
Co-Lead Pastor of Capital City Church
Founder, Beautiful You Movement

Introduction

THE SECRET OF
THE METHOD

HAVE YOU EVER TRIED TO LOSE WEIGHT and wound up frustrated, exhausted, and feeling intense disappointment? Have you ever wrestled with pain that seems to live so deep it seems indescribable?

Have you ever been confused about why you can't seem to make progress and it seems like you're just hitting a wall?

I know I have.

On one occasion I was experiencing so much frustration trying to lose weight, I remember hitting my forehead so hard against my mirror, that it left a ringing in my ears!

I hated what I saw.

I would shoot daggers of disappointment at my chin. Eye-beam lasers of liposuction at my thighs.

When negative self-talk is the soundtrack of your existence and your morning hangover is the sting of yesterday's failures … it's difficult to know how to divorce disorder from one's soul.

Caught up among eating disorders and plaguing insecurity, I was desperate for a way out. I poured over hundreds of books and even sought a degree in health looking for the answers that could provide me relief.

Nothing worked.

The only advice offered for overcoming my insecurities was to "just get over it." I didn't have a clue as to how to do that! I'd be pumped up by hearing: "You can do it!" and "Love yourself!" Yet, within the hour, I'd be accosted by negative thoughts.

I needed a strategy.

I needed something to do.

I needed to fight fear with a plan.

In this book, I'm going to lay out the keys that brought me wholeness and deep-seated contentedness … and even how I lost 35 pounds as a result.

Rather than a meal plan or exercise regime, *The Brave*

Body Method is a simple but proven strategy that says you must become brave first in your mind, before you can experience success in your physical body.

The Brave Body Method will enable you to finally discover your worth and seize the authority you've been given to become free from disabling addictions to food, negative self-talk, and emotional eating.

> The bravest thing you can do is lay down the crippling self-loathing and finally start loving yourself the way God intends.

For the bravest thing you can do is lay down the crippling self-loathing and finally start loving yourself the way God intends. Stop the madness of inferior thinking, and start seeing yourself as the hot, strong, well-able Son or Daughter of the Most High.

The secret sauce of *The Brave Body Method* is this:

By getting brave on the inside, you will unlock the secret to feeling better about yourself, causing all the outward effects of health to fall into place: losing weight, gaining confidence, and finding renewed vitality.

And guess what? You absolutely can do this. And this is your time.

As a pastor and lifetime student of health, I've become addicted to wellness of the total package: mind, body, and spirit. I have spent over 15 years reading hundreds of books and research articles on these topics. I've boiled it down to this four-step plan to get you from frustration to freedom by finally discovering your worth through God's eyes.

These are the truths that caused practical results in my own life, distilled succinctly into a concise, easy-to-read format.

Leonardo Da Vinci said, "Simplicity is the ultimate sophistication." In that spirit, *The Brave Body Method* is a clear, actionable guide to jump-start your new body image, lose the pounds, and ignite your faith along the way.

By the end of The Method, you'll feel lighter and more confident in your body. You'll find your faith stronger than ever, along with an increased self-discipline that will carry into all aspects of your life.

What is the real secret to feeling better?

AN EPIDEMIC OF DISORDER

A research study found on average, women have 13 negative body thoughts daily—nearly one for every waking hour, and 97% of women admit to having at least one "I hate my body" moment each day![1]

I know I sure did.

> 97% of women admit to having at least one "I hate my body" moment each day.

Negative self-talk affects our self-esteem, our relationships, and our entire physiology. Most importantly, our confidence plummets, and we have no energy to go after our dreams and goals.

Worse, we already know everything we are doing wrong. We know we need to:

Eat better.

Exercise more.

Be less stressed.

When it comes to health and our bodies, our problem isn't about knowing what to do. Our problem is finding out how to feel better about ourselves in order to do those things.

Surrounded by self-help programs, fad diets, juice cleanses, eating plans, and exercise regimes, the myriad of options is overwhelming. Thousands of books have been written with themes such as "Eat Low Carb," or "Do These 5 Routines For a Bum as Hard as Your Driveway!"

What we haven't realized is that for our body to experience lasting change, it must be healthy from the inside out. Cracking the code of "getting inside" ourselves is the only thing that can bring the deeper, lasting results we crave.

This is **not** a diet plan.
This is a "die to your old thinking" plan.

This may not be for you … this is not a diet plan.

This is a "die to your old thinking" plan.

Because this isn't about skinny, it's about healthy. True wellness has never been the size jeans you wear, but the soundness of your soul.

In my experience, people don't have a lot of time to research the practical strategies that will work, so I've included a daily action plan that will have you seeing results right away. You'll also discover:

- *Scripture Lists and Posters* for you to stay motivated
- *Easy Exercises* you can start implementing immediately
- *A Daily Action Guide* to jump-start your wellness

Before we begin, I want to share with you the revelation that lit a fire in me and began causing "brave" to shoot through my spine. Ready?

STOP HIDING AND START ACTING AS IF WHAT GOD SAYS ABOUT YOU IS TRUE

This idea is what finally started causing results. After years of studying, reading, and listening to messages daily, I was able to boil it down to this granular truth. I had to stop avoiding the truth of who God made me and "act as if" I already had the discipline, confidence, and authority that He said I could have.

I needed to start acting as if I was God's masterpiece RIGHT NOW. And so are you![2]

That's the secret.

Successful weight loss and gaining a healthy body image starts happening when you confidently act on God's word.

It's the same thing as shopping a sale.

> God wants you to rise up and
> bravely take Him at His Word.

Imagine getting a coupon advertising "Jeans 50% off!" in the mail. Even if you arrived at the store and didn't see the discount on the tag, you would confidently walk to the register, coupon in hand, acting as if what the coupon said you could have was yours.

Once you stop hiding and show up in life putting a

demand on God's Promises, then you will have what He says you can have. That's what God wants! He wants you to bravely take Him at His Word. He wants to see you feeling great and moving confidently in the direction of your dreams.[3]

Let's get moving because this is going to be a great journey, and I can't WAIT till you experience the liberty, hope, and freedom that belong to you!

KISS METHOD

The Method is based on the acronym KISS because it's broken down into simple steps.

The KISS Principle is a term coined by a US Navy aircraft engineer, Kelly Johnson for:
"Keep it simple, stupid."

The principle hails that most systems work best if simplicity is the goal and avoiding unnecessary complexities at all cost.

4 STEPS TO GAIN SELF-ACCEPTANCE & WIN THE WAR ON WEIGHT

STEP 1:
"K"

KNOW YOU ARE HOT
You Are What You Think You Are

God wants you to know how valuable you really are. In this step, you will grab hold of the fact that you are a God-Pod and learn how thoughts become things, so you must choose the best ones.

STEP 2:
"I"

INFLICT DAMAGE
Speak Only What You Seek

Second, you must learn there is a miracle in your mouth waiting to be released. If the battle is in your mind, the weapons are in your whispers.

STEP 3:
"S"
SEE THE GOD-PAINTING
Vision Board For Your Soul

Learn how to embrace the "God-Painting" of your future. Harness the untapped vision board of your mind, and "see" inside before you "see" outside.

STEP 4:
"S"
START BEFORE YOU ARE READY
Act As If

Too often we take action without being positioned properly in faith. So often we're trying to move a giant tree, and God is just asking us to plant a seed. You do what you can, and God will do what you cannot.

To grab a free downloadable workbook that will guide you through these steps, please visit www.bravebodymethod.com.

STEP 1

"K"

KNOW YOU ARE HOT

1

Excuse Me, Your Behind is in the Way

What lies behind you and what lies in front of you,
pales in comparison to what lies inside of you.
—RALPH WALDO EMERSON

"COULD YOU KINDLY MOVE YOUR BEHIND PLEASE?"
"What was ... that?" I exclaimed, spinning around to address the voice.

It was then I realized my rear end was in the way, keeping the man from his table. Recognizing the hilarity of the situation, we both erupted in laughter, causing looks of irritation from those grabbing lunch around us.

Having just delivered my third child, I was 60 pounds over my normal weight. In my present state, I was unaware of my new body dimensions. Granted, my bottom was much rounder than normal, but in a strange phenomenon unique to childbearing, it had also grown horizontally.

It was as if a small shelf was now attached to my backside. Why, the man could have rested his coffee on my behind if he had wanted to!

In that moment, it was as if time stood still. The lyric of the laughter, the aghast look on the gentleman's face—life played in surreal slow motion as I contemplated:

I hadn't always been as kind to my body as I was being now. In fact, we had been vicious enemies for over two decades.

The moment lasted only seconds, but within the sound of the laughter was the echo of my freedom. I recognized something profound in this corner bistro, something that had eluded me throughout my youth:

I had finally made peace with my behind.

When what lies behind you is disappointment with your weight or frustration that you just can't seem to move forward—it's easy to let what's behind you, define you.

As a 20-year-old, I had been so long involved with disordered eating that I began to believe disorder was my future.

I couldn't imagine a world where I would wake up and not obsess about my body or what I was eating.

I couldn't imagine living light and free, devoid of the aching insecurity and depression that had become my constant companions.

I desperately wanted to experience a different reality, but I had no idea how.

My big behind was in the way.

It was as if there lay a chasm between who I longed to be—healthy, radiant, secure, confident—and who I saw in the mirror. All I saw was a girl that was overweight and unstable, with a side of cray-cray.

I simply could not figure out how to cross this chasm of impossibility, how to find the invisible bridge to my potential that would lead me to become who I wanted to be.

Have you ever felt like it would take a miracle to get you to your destiny?

CHASM CROSSING

If you close your eyes, you can almost sense your best life. With eyes closed, there you are: confident, brave, full of health, brimming with wellness, energy, and purpose.

When you open your eyes, it's as if there is a chasm between this ideal picture and what you see in the mirror. As

29

William James said, "Compared to what we ought to be, we are only half awake." We can sense our potential for a healthier, braver version of ourselves just waiting in the distance.

> "Compared to what we ought to be, we are only half awake." —William James

However, when faced with the distance to our destination, the gap between where we are presently and who we want to be permanently can seem insurmountable. Before we know it, we can fall into discouraging, depressing, and disillusioning thoughts such as:

- "It's all so overwhelming ..."
- "I'll never lose ALL the weight I have to ..."
- "I blew it yesterday, so why even try today?"

Until you learn how to actively engage in God's promises for your life, you are in danger of staying stuck on one side of the chasm. There are limitless possibilities on the other side. Your strong healthy body and your confident self lie across the chasm. They are yours for the taking, but you must cooperate with the miraculous power of God to get across.

In the Bible, the Israelites were faced with an enormous chasm to cross. They were in the land of Canaan, heading to the Promised Land. The Israelites were facing a chasm of giants, insurmountable rivers, and enemy combatants desiring to kill them.

Yep, they were slightly hesitant.

This was like the Grand Canyon of impossibility.

God was telling them to GO and that He would be with them every step of the way—but frankly, it didn't make sense to them. In a striking move of sanctioned mediocrity, the Israelites refused to go forward.

In a striking move of sanctioned mediocrity,
the Israelites refused to go forward.

Because the Israelites couldn't enlarge their thinking, they found themselves missing out on the wild, beautiful adventure God intended for them. Over 1,078,000 people died, wandering and still wondering[4] what was on the other side of their chasm. The Bible gravely calls their negative thinking an "evil heart of unbelief."[5]

God called it "unbelief" when the Israelites could not accept: *That they were who He said they were. That they could do what He said they could do.*

"Unbelief" is what kept the Israelites out of the Promised Land and what causes you and me to stay broken-down,

31

busted, disgusted, and on the side of the road toward our best body. God was calling the Israelites toward greatness, but because they could not shake off their inferior mindset, they did not walk in their superior identity in Him.

They were hiding. They were allowing what was behind them to define them.

> Until you begin to RISE up and stop hiding
> from the greatness God is calling you to,
> you will not experience the awesome fullness
> of God's best for you.

Until you begin to RISE up and stop hiding from the greatness God is calling you to, you will not experience the awesome fullness of God's best for you. Knowing who you are, and whose you are, is the key to crossing the chasm.

You are so precious and beloved by God, He wants to be SO close in fact, that you become "… a body wholly filled and flooded with God Himself!"[6]

God wants your body and your entire life filled with His presence, His vitality, and His freedom. He wants you to feel so good you pinch yourself in the morning!

It's interesting that of the million or so Israelites in the desert, only two people from the original generation crossed the chasm. Only Joshua and Caleb choose to see themselves as who God said they were: *Land-Takers. Dominion-Dwellers. Brave Bodies.*

You are so precious and beloved by God.
He wants to be SO close in fact,
that you become a body wholly filled and
flooded with God Himself.

Joshua and Caleb believed that there might be pain in the conquering, but it would beat the pain of remaining, any day of the week. In the same way, there is only pain if you remain ...

- If you remain in the past, *there is pain.*
- If you remain in your old patterns of thinking, *there is pain.*
- If you remain in your comfort zone of disbelief, *there is pain.*

But strength arises when you choose to step forward, determined to possess your God-given worth and value.

You can be just like Joshua and Caleb!

Determine that you *will* get across that chasm, and believe you are who God says you are and have everything He says you can have. This is why I called this *The Brave Body Method*—because until we rise up, bravely believing we are the hot, well-able Sons and Daughters of the Most-High … we'll just stay stuck on our "behinds."

I read that prior to battle, the Tartar tribes of Central Asia used to make a pronouncement over their enemies. It had nothing to do with their ability to overpower or wipe out their enemy in battle. Instead their curse was: "May you stay in one place forever."

That's what the Enemy desires for you—to stay just the same this year as you were last year. Determine to come up higher in your thinking and whatever it costs you—to become who God has called you to be.

"You don't have to be great to start, but you do have to start to be great." —Zig Ziglar

---

While it took me years to apprehend the keys to move forward, you are going to move much faster. Zig Ziglar said, "You don't have to be great to start, but you do have to start to be great."

Let's discover who you really are.

2

YOU ARE WHAT YOU THINK YOU ARE

The good Lord gave you a body that can stand most anything.
It's your mind you have to convince.

—VINCE LOMBARDI

D O YOU EVER THINK OF THE "IT" GIRL from high school? Remember her? The girl who always seemed to emanate easy, breezy, beautiful cover-girl coolness? Hair and makeup perfect?

Yeah, she went to my school, too.

Her name was Veronica, and amazingly enough, she let me hang out with her. I was so insecure, my sense of self-esteem would rise just being around her. I felt important. As sophomores, I still remember how goofy the guys in my class would act around her. They were so oblivious to their inane antics, just to get her to look in their direction.

I *so* wanted to be her.

There was just one problem, I was NOT her. I spent a lot of time wasting valuable energy to alter my personality to be just a little bit more "mysterious" like her and to get my giggle just spot-on to resemble hers.

While walking one day with her along our high school campus, we walked by a large school bus that we didn't realize was filled with the boys' lacrosse team. This team was noted amongst us girls as having the best-looking, most athletic young men in our school. No, this was not the chess team; these guys were the crème de la crème. The hotties. Superstars.

To pass by a *few* of the lacrosse team would cause any sophomore girl's heart to race. Here we were passing the *entire* team on the bus. Soon the seniors started yelling out, "Hey, Veronica! Veronica!"

She looked over casually and coolly and gave the smile and nod. (I swear I saw some of them drooling.) I studied her closely, taking notes on how to be her ... And then it happened—*smack!* The next thing I remember was the blue sky above.

While I was taking notes on how to be Veronica, I failed to see the oncoming lamppost.

If I close my eyes, I can still hear the sound of 35 good-looking young men laughing.

If you don't know who *you* are,
all you're going to do is stumble.

Ladies, here is the moral of this story: If you don't know who *you* are, all you're going to do is stumble.

In fact, the Scripture says we should not "look and speak and act the same."[7] We need to find who God has made us each uniquely to be. For how we perceive ourselves is the key to unlocking our potential.

E. E. Cummings said, "To be nobody but yourself in a world that's doing its best to make you somebody else, is to fight the hardest battle you are ever going to fight. Never stop fighting." In this chapter we're going to discover the power of your thoughts. You're going to learn how thoughts become things, so choosing God's highest and best thoughts toward you is vital.

You'll also discover how you aren't your weak moments; you are your peak moments. Through practicing this step once a day, you will learn to harness the power of a renewed mind to achieve a transformed body.

THOUGHTS BECOME THINGS

Everything can be traced back to a thought. Everything begins in the mind. *Mascara. iPhones. Reese's Peanut Butter Cups. Chanel. Starbucks!* As Stephen Covey wrote in the iconic *7 Habits of Highly Successful People,* everything we see is an act of "second creation."[8]

As Stephen Covey wrote, "Everything we see is an act of "second creation." The first creation has **always** been in the mind.

The first creation has *always* been in the mind.

If we are creating with our mind, it follows that our minds are radically affecting our health, right now. In fact, research shows approximately 87% of illnesses can be attributed to our thought life, and only 13% to diet, genetics and environment.[9]

Research shows that fear triggers more than 1,400 known

physical and chemical responses and activates more than 30 different hormones and neurotransmitters. In turn, these hormones directly impact weight gain, confidence, and just about every other bodily function![10]

87% of illnesses can be attributed to our thought life, and only 13% to diet, genetics and environment.

The Bible echoes this truth when it declares how thoughts become *things:*

> *As a man thinks in his heart, so is he.*
> —Proverbs 23:7 NKJV

This Scripture teaches that *your life* is a reflection of your thoughts. You are actually *becoming* what you think about!

Digging into the Hebrew, the Scripture above actually translates, "As he is all along in his heart so is he at *last,* in his actions." Our actions are just outplaying what's *already occurred* in our minds. We are seeing "on the outside" what we believe to be true "on the inside."

Therefore, a healthy body image isn't a physical one, it's a mental one.

The secret conversations you hold in the privacy of your own mind are shaping your health, little by little. So it follows that if you want to change your way of living, you need to change your way of thinking.

> The secret conversations you hold in the privacy of your own mind are shaping your health, little by little.

As Henry Ford has famously once said:

"Whether you think you can or think you can't—you're right."

- If you think you are a person of discipline, then *you will be.*

- If you begin to see yourself as healthy and energetic, then *you will be.*

- If you believe your body can lose weight easily, then *you will.*

How can we actually get inside our minds and change our thoughts?

The Scripture gives us the key to lasting change, when it says:

> *Be transformed by the renewal of your mind.*
> —Romans 12:2 ESV

If we could unpack *how* to renew our mind, we could in fact transform our body, gain self-acceptance, and discover our unique God-given identity. Renewing our mind doesn't have to be painful or mysterious.

In the next chapter we'll break down how to actually get rid of negative self-talk, so you can feed consistently on powerful truths that will effortlessly release your potential.

3

THE 4:8 FILTER

Yesterday is gone. Tomorrow has not yet come.
We have only today. Let us begin.

—MOTHER TERESA

BENJAMIN DISRAELI SAID, "Nurture great thoughts, for you will never go higher than your thoughts." In order to think God's thoughts, we need to find out what we *should* be thinking. The Bible gives us a great "To Think" List in Philippians 4:8.

"Nurture great thoughts, for you will never go higher than your thoughts." —Benjamin Disraeli

---

OUR "TO THINK" LIST

> *Finally, brothers and sisters, whatever is true,*
> *whatever is noble, whatever is right,*
> *whatever is pure, whatever is lovely,*
> *whatever is admirable—if anything is excellent*
> *or praiseworthy, think about such things.*
> —Philippians 4:8 NIV

In order to renew your mind, you need to filter your thoughts through the 4:8 strainer. For a moment, picture a white, plastic spaghetti strainer on top of your head. Pretend for a day that you only let what is noble, right, pure, and excellent into your brain.

All other negative, unhelpful information is unable to penetrate through the holes of the strainer. Can you imagine how uplifted, encouraging, and productive your day might be?

This is the goal when the Scripture says, "Think about such things." Or as the Amplified version says, "*Fix* your minds on them."

Get a FIX on what is amazing about you.

Get a fix on your best qualities and your unique gifts. For no one on the planet can replicate what you add, what you bring, and how you do it!

Too often we let negative thoughts sabotage our mind and fall into our head. Rather than fixing our mind on the good, we often fixate on the negative. In fact, we often do the reverse of this scripture, as if it read: *Finally, whatever is untrue, dishonest, unjust, impure, ugly, negative, vicious, or worthy of criticism—think about these things.*

10 UGLY, HAIRY THOUGHTS

1. *I'm fat.*

2. *I'm ugly.*

3. *I don't have what it takes.*

4. *I used to have so much energy.*

5. *I could never do that.*

6. *I just look at dessert, and I gain weight.*

7. *It's hopeless.*

8. *I'm too old to do that.*

9. *I'm too busy.*

10. *I'm always overwhelmed.*

If we do in fact "become what we are thinking about," we must learn the habit of continually fixing our minds on what is good and true about who God says we are.

I love what author Tommy Newberry says in the book, *The 4:8 Principle*, "Instead of exhaustively re-describing your problems, the [Philippians] 4:8 principle counsels you to marinate in the solutions to your problems."

Remember, *thoughts become things,* so choosing positive thoughts would be far more productive.

10 HOT THOUGHTS

1. *I am healthy and vibrant.*

2. *I plan my meals and snacks.*

3. *My metabolism works effectively.*

4. *I have more than enough energy.*

5. *I crave lean protein, healthy carbs, and essential fats.*

6. *I drink lots of pure water.*

7. *I am free of addictions and destructive lifestyle habits.*

8. *I can do it through Christ.*

9. *I lose weight easily.*

10. *My best days are still ahead of me.*

You may not be able to control your circumstances, but you can unquestioningly control what you choose to dwell on. When you do, you will find the external circumstances of weight, self-image, and confidence take care of themselves.

The primary way we fix our minds is to continually bring our minds back to the 4:8 Filter. The goal is weighing each thought against the criteria in Paul's list.

- *Is this thought good?*
- *Is this thought pure?*
- *Is this thought praise-worthy?*

You may be thinking that this sounds like a lot of work. It *is.*

But it won't take you long to realize that it's actually *less* work than all the emotional energy you have been expending on negative self-talk! Those negative thoughts have brought you undue worry, fear, fatigue—and are exhausting you little by little.

In contrast, when you begin choosing good thoughts they will produce good things—peace, love, serenity, and the life you've been craving.

Remember that every moment, every thought, is a choice. This means *each moment is a new beginning.* Choose the good over the evil. Choose to think positive, hot thoughts, and your body will respond accordingly.

> Every moment, every thought, is a choice.
> Each moment is a new beginning.

Begin right now by switching over to thinking "4:8," ask yourself these questions:

- *What are my five most amazing qualities?*
- *What are five things I love about my body?*

As you get a fix on thinking 4:8—get ready to start experiencing "masterpiece moments"—glimpses of the real you! More about that in the next chapter.

4

YOU ARE A
MASTERPIECE

*You shall also be [so beautiful and prosperous as
to be thought of as] a crown of glory and honor in the
hand of the Lord, and a royal diadem [exceedingly beautiful]
in the hand of your God.*

—ISAIAH 62:3-5

S O OFTEN WE LIVE THINKING THAT WE ARE a little
piece of disaster when, in fact, God calls us His
"masterpiece."

For we are God's masterpiece.
He has created us anew in Christ Jesus,
so we can do the good things he planned for us long ago.
—Ephesians 2:10 NLT

A "masterpiece" refers to an artist's largest, and perhaps best, greatest, most popular, or most renowned achievement. In our modern day usage, the word "masterpiece" denotes luxury, rarity, and ingenuity.

So often we live thinking we're a little piece of disaster when, in fact, God calls us His "masterpiece."

There is an annual international fair in London called "Masterpiece" which hosts the rarest art, antiques, and designs. Recent standout items included:

- A Roy Lichtenstein painting called "Puzzle Portrait" valued at $20 million

- A pearl once owned by Mary Tudor, 64.5 carats, valued at more than $11 million

- A 1925 first-edition *The Great Gatsby* by F. Scott Fitzgerald valued at $178 million

In this collection the estimation of the item is determined by the caliber of the original artist. If the world considers these masterpieces, valuing these items for millions of dollars, and your original artist is God—how much more are you worth?

> You are the work of God, His hottest,
> most luxurious creation!
> You are the pinnacle of His creation,
> the apex of all His works.

You are the work of God, His hottest, most luxurious creation! You are the pinnacle of His creation, the apex of all His works.

The word for "masterpiece" in the Greek is *poiēma* from which we get the English word "poem." It means expressive art. You are God's passionate expression in this world; you are a masterpiece! *Hold your head up high*—you are not a disaster-piece, you are His masterpiece.

Try this next exercise to "fix your mind" on God's Word.

YOU ARE YOUR MASTERPIECE MOMENTS

Think of a recent "masterpiece" moment, a time when everything went better than you had hoped and you felt your best.

Maybe it was a time when you woke up early, hit the gym, or didn't overdo it at the buffet and demonstrated magnificent self-control.

Perhaps it was when you were recognized for that achievement, the performance went better than you hoped, the outfit looked better than expected!

Got one in mind?

What happens is we often *disregard* these experiences as good luck, as if it's a "masquerader" who came, hijacked our schedule, exceeded expectations, and then magically left our body.

This "masquerader complex" will rob us of our moment.

- *I must have gotten great rest last night; I wish I could do that every time.*

- *I wish I could eat healthy more often, but I can't help it.*

- *That was weird! I guess I'm having a rare moment.*

The "masquerader" is an inner voice that tries to persuade you that despite evidence to the contrary, you are playing over your head. Instead of savoring the Masterpiece Moment, you dissolve the breakthrough. Instead of defining yourself by your Masterpiece Moments, you define yourself by your disaster moments.

But a girl who knows she is HOT, will shake it off, attributing those disaster moments instead to the "masquerader":

- *I know I usually do better than that.*

- *I know I usually am amazing at that. I didn't hit it this time, but no worries.*

- *That's not like me!*

We over-identify with our *failings* and
under-identify with our *victories*.

We over-identify with our *failings* and under-identify with our *victories*.

The truth is, when you appear to be playing over your head, you are actually glimpsing **your full potential.** Why not choose to see that event, that time you excelled, that moment when the earth and heaven collided, *as who you really are?*

You need to over-identify with these experiences and think on what is lovely, true, gracious, and worthy of praise about *you.*

Here's the truth: your greatest Masterpiece Moments are you. Yet in reality, they still pale in comparison to the true identity you have in God. Your best days are only glimpses of who God has really made you to be!

Your best days are only glimpses of who God has really made you to be!

In fact, you are such a masterpiece of design, so precious to God, that He actually wants to move in—to you. In the next chapter, discover how proper self-care is holiness and how to treat your God-Pod with the respect it deserves.

To grab a free "Know You're Hot" two-part video training, please visit www.bravebodymethod.com.

5

YOU ARE A GOD-POD

Dear God, My prayer for this year is that you give me a
fat bank account and a thin body. Please don't
mix these up like you did last year.
—ANONYMOUS

IT MAY BE HARD TO BELIEVE, but the Scripture actually teaches that you are God's housing, the dwelling place for His awesome Presence. In the book of Corinthians, Paul writes:

> *Or do you not know that your body is a temple of the*
> *Holy Spirit who is in you, whom you have from God,*
> *and that you are not your own?*
> —1 Corinthians 6:19 NASB

Christian scholar and author N. T. Wright explains: "To Western Christians, thinking anachronistically of the temple as simply the Jewish equivalent of a cathedral, the image is simply one metaphor among many and without much apparent significance."[11]

It's tempting to glide over the fact that our physical bodies are meant to house God's power. If you have been in Christian circles, you may have heard the common admonition to "ask Jesus into your heart." However, this was a revolutionary concept when Paul wrote this passage. It had only been 25 years since the Crucifixion of Christ, and the Jewish temple in Jerusalem was still standing.

Paul's earth-shattering revelation is this: the same magnificent, majestic, miraculous glory of God who had inhabited this glorious physical building, was meant to inhabit Jesus himself and his people—you.

To the Jewish people this was radical. Mind-blowing. Scandalous. God in your body?

You are a God-Pod.

Yes, you are made to be a God-Pod.

As Pope John Paul II declared in his *Theology of the Body:*

"The body, and it alone, is capable of making visible what is invisible, spiritual and divine. [The body] was created to transfer into the visible reality, the invisible mystery hidden in God from time immemorial, and thus to be a sign of it. [The body] is the fundamental fact of human existence."[12]

Self-care can thus be placed soundly within our theology. Self-care is not selfish; it is a form of holiness. Your human body is one of the greatest gifts you will ever receive from God. YOU are the sacred space where He dwells. You are therefore worth caring for.

The concept of self-care is not new. According to an account of Hillel the Elder, an iconic Jewish religious leader who lived in the first century BC, "after bidding farewell to his disciples, he kept walking along with them. His disciples asked him, 'Master, where are you going?'

He replied, 'To do a good turn to a guest in my house.'

They said, 'Every day you seem to have a guest.'

He replied, 'Is not my poor soul a guest in my body, here today and tomorrow here no longer?'"[13]

This sentiment is seen again in the wisdom books, "The merciful man does good to his own soul: but he that is cruel troubles his own flesh."[14] The idea of self-care is also found in the New Testament, *"For no man ever hated his own flesh, but nourishes and carefully protects and cherishes it."*[15]

Nourishes.

Protects.

Cherishes.

These are not words we commonly use when referring to our health. Yet, these are the words that describe how God desires YOU to treat yourself. We cannot escape the idea that we need to take care of this one and only Temple.

This idea comes from God Himself.

How have you been treating your Temple?

See your everyday life—your eating, exercising, rest, recreation—as a sacred honor. You are taking God with you wherever you go.

Treat your body like a God-Pod. This means seeing your everyday life—your eating, exercising, rest, recreation—as a sacred honor. You are taking God with you wherever you go.

Be patient with yourself.

Treat yourself kindly.

Speak to yourself like a cherished friend.

Next, let's explore what actually is happening when we

don't treat ourselves with the dignity, respect, and honor God desires. In the next chapter learn how to permanently defeat negative self-talk, and posture yourself for maximum breakthrough.

6

YOU ARE A TARGET

*Don't think of Satan as a harmless cartoon character with
a red suit and a pitchfork. He is very clever and powerful,
and his unchanging purpose is to defeat God's plans at
every turn, including His plans for your life.*

—BILLY GRAHAM

O N MARCH 18, 1990, TWO COPS RANG the doorbell
at the Isabelle Stewart Gardener Museum in Boston.
The night watchman on duty was a young, new
employee named Rick Albath. After he buzzed them in, the
cops said to him and the other guard working with him,
"Gentlemen, this is a robbery."

That night the two thieves, dressed as police officers, stole 13 pieces of art. Among the works were three Rembrandt's, a Vermeer, a Manet, and sketches by Degas.[16] The collective worth of the works was over $500 million dollars. The crime is hailed as the most famous art heist in history.

> As a masterpiece and a God-Pod, you must recognize that you are also a target.

The moral of the story is this: Great masterpieces are simultaneously treasures *and* targets.

As a masterpiece and a God-Pod, you must recognize that you are also a target.

MASTERPIECE HEIST

Whether you know it or not, there's a war over your life, a bull's-eye on your back, and a hit list with your name on it.

Have you ever experienced a vague feeling of resistance?

Or felt it overwhelmingly challenging, just to get through ordinary life?

Did it seem like an unseen Enemy was at work against you?

If so, I'm here to confirm you were right!

The Bible teaches there is an Enemy of our souls.[17] His

primary mission is to keep you from experiencing God's best for your life by tormenting your mind.[18]

He'll tee up thoughts of discouragement, disappointment, and condemnation **24 hours a day** if you let him.

His primary goal?

Your self-sabotage, in the form of negative self-talk.

> The Enemy knows if he can get you to focus on your failings, you will absolutely forfeit your future.

The Enemy knows if he can get you to focus on your failings, you will absolutely forfeit your future. When he tempted Eve in the garden, his aim was to get her to see "she was naked." Only THEN did she hide in fear, condemnation, and shame.

His influence got her to focus on her *lack—what she didn't have*. That is what drove her into darkness and into hiding. She was a masterpiece, hijacked by negative self-talk. The Enemy wants to steal your potential by getting you to become your OWN worst enemy.

I know I certainly was!

I listened to the soundtrack of berating, criticizing, and self-loathing so much I was worn out from morning to night.

YOU ARE NOT YOUR NEGATIVE SELF-TALK

Before I experienced freedom, I remember seeing a photograph of myself captured during a night out with friends. It was a great big group shot, but my eyes zeroed in on my button-down blue chambray shirt.

Between the buttons, every 2 inches, a little "peek" of my white, blubbery skin emerged. The buttons were literally popping wide-open. Up until that time, I had *no idea* I had gained that much weight. Looking at this photograph, disgust rippled through me ... the pain was visceral and real.

I began the mental soundtrack—I guess this is who I am. *Overweight, average, unattractive.*

My body was suffering under the load of extra weight and excess burden. The chaos of eating disorders, both anorexia and then bulimia, were causing me to experience amenorrhea, the cessation of my period.

The real crisis came when my doctor told me if I didn't begin to get healthy, I could be unable to become pregnant.

I was so discouraged.

I figured that if I was **this** frustrated
with myself, God must be too.

I figured that if I was *this* frustrated with myself, God must be too. I needed a breakthrough, but I first needed to stop confusing my ravaged emotional state for how God felt about me.

All too easily, we allow our emotions to dictate our theology, rather than elevating our thinking to match God's character. Christa Black, author of *God Loves Ugly*, says it like this, "If you are not anchored in the goodness of God, you will lower your theology to match your pain."

"If you are not anchored in the goodness of God, you will lower your theology to match your pain." —Christa Black

---

In order to elevate my life, I needed to recognize that my negative self-talk was actually the very thing preventing my breakthrough.

What brought new understanding was discovering that this obsessive focus on my weight was actually a heavy reliance on myself. The light bulb came on when I read James Chapter 4 and saw how disorder arises:

What leads to strife [discord and feuds] and how do conflicts [quarrels and fighting] originate among you? ... You burn with envy and anger and are not able to obtain [the gratification, the contentment, and the happiness that you seek], so you fight and war ...

*Do you not know that being the world's friend is being God's enemy? ... **God sets Himself against the proud** and haughty, but gives grace[continually] to the lowly [those who are humble enough to receive it].*
—James 4:1-6

This passage teaches us that relying on oneself instead of God causes an internal war.

In reading this passage, I began to understand that *pride* was keeping the flow of God's power (grace) from flooding into my soul. All the frustration, the incessant negative self-talk, was actually ME trying to fix me.

It was actually pride! And—yikes—pride was positioning me squarely against my answer—God Himself!

God and I were on opposite teams?!

This was why I had been experiencing the epitome of frustration. Though I hadn't realized it, by using my efforts alone, I was completely focused on me. God, my Creator and Savior, was forgotten.

NEGATIVE SELF-TALK IS ACTUALLY PRIDE

Simply put, pride is you looking at YOU to meet your needs.

The spotlight is on you, evaluating your achievements.

Your appearance.

Your self-worth.

You are the center of your thought life.

When you rely on yourself, you effectively
deny God's supernatural ability.

An over-obsession with self is impeding your break-through. When you rely on yourself, you effectively deny God's supernatural ability. Paul echoes this sentiment when he *pleads* with us to not "nullify the grace of God."[19]

We make the grace of God of no effect when we self-select ourselves out by reliance upon our self-effort.

The Hebrew King David wrote, "In his pride the wicked does not seek him; in all his thoughts there is no room for God."[20]

> *Be subject to God. **Resist the devil** [stand firm*
> *against him], and he will flee from you.*
> —James 4:7

How do we win over this pride and unhealthy self-consciousness?

You can win, but only through rejecting your self-effort and resting in who *He says you are.*

You can win, but only through rejecting your self-effort and resting in who *He says you are.*

OVERCOMING SELF CONSCIOUSNESS

This lesson was highlighted to me when once, when I was out shopping. I was six months pregnant with my second child, and feeling SO uncomfortable with my body. I remember a man saying:

"Are you carrying twins?"

"No," I replied.

"You must be about to deliver any day though … right?" said the Surly Man.

I had 3 more months to go.

I'm large. I get it. I wanted to say: "Did you know pregnant women gain weight? It's this funny thing that happens when you are BUSY CONVERTING FOOD INTO A TINY HUMAN."

I remember being surprised because the man's comment didn't sting like it once would have. Though I felt uncomfortable, I was not plagued by self-consciousness as I was before my healing.

I remember what it felt like to think about my body and food constantly. I remember being so controlled by my weight I couldn't imagine ever being free.

Have you ever been at war? but with yourself?

One of the keys to ending my internal war was reading a book called *You are Not What you Weigh* by Lisa Bevere. For the first time, I saw how my weight had become an "idol" in my life. She beautifully unveiled the solution when she wrote:

> *"The opposite of self conscious is not a 'good' self image or self esteem. The opposite of conscious is unconscious. To lose consciousness of one's self happens when we become more conscious or aware of God and His will, than we are of self, and its will."*

The key was this: Decrease unhealthy consciousness of myself, and heighten my consciousness of God. After reading this, something literally broke off of me in my life.

EXCHANGE SELF-CONSCIOUSNESS FOR GOD CONSCIOUSNESS

True humility is laying down what you think and rising up to what God thinks. As the great pastor and author Andrew

Murray commented, "Pride must die in you, or nothing of heaven can live in you." If frustration is what you feel, it's meant to drive you into the arms of the Grace-giving God.

If you are overwhelmed, exhausted, and hitting the limits of your *own* power, I have great news! You're NOW eligible to step into *His*.

Abandon relying on yourself, and recognize it's not YOU but God who's going to do the work. For "the things which are impossible with men are possible with God."[21]

After doing *The Brave Body Method* for three months, I finally went to the scale in my bathroom, which I had not looked at since I had started. My jaw flat-out dropped to the floor, and I started crying!

I had reached my goal weight!

While losing the weight was significant, I had gained so much more. I cried because I felt, for the very first time, I was living in the middle of a miracle.

Yes, my jeans were looser.

Yes, my confidence was soaring.

Yes, my depression was lifting.

But real reward was that the warm embers of faith in a *living* God had been stoked within my heart.

This goal of heartfelt reliance on God is why James admonishes us to submit to God, to resist the negative self-talk and dependence on self-effort. Not ONLY will we see the Enemy flee, but we will become recipients of the greatest gift of all: *God's never ending river of grace, love, and power.*

Soon, one morning I woke up to find my period had returned. You've never seen a girl so on fire to have her period! I was ecstatic.

Miracles are happening all around you.

Cease the negative self-talk.

Come to the end of yourself and your self-effort.

Respond to this glorious message of Grace. You are who God says you are!

A PRAYER

Make me brave to see myself as you see me.
Help me have the humility to believe what you
say about me. Forgive me for looking to myself
and not You to do the work,
and forgive my pride and negative self-talk.
I give up! Do what only You can do God.
In Jesus' Name, Amen.

STEP 1 FUN SHEETS

What is an ugly, hairy, thought you have been having lately?

_____

_____

_____

What are five of your most amazing qualities?

1. _____ 2. _____

3. _____ 4. _____ 5. _____

What are five things you love about your body?

1. _____ 2. _____

3. _____ 4. _____ 5. _____

If you spoke to yourself as a cherished friend, what would you say?

_____

_____

_____

_____

What is one of your "masterpiece" moments, a time when everything went better than you had hoped and you felt at your absolute BEST?

_____

_____

_____

What is one *Hot Thought* you can begin to think upon?

1. I am healthy and vibrant.
2. I plan my meals and snacks.
3. My metabolism works effectively.
4. I have more than enough energy.
5. I crave lean protein, healthy carbs, and essential fats.
6. I drink lots of pure water.
7. I am on top of addictions and destructive lifestyle habits.
8. I can do it through Christ.
9. I lose weight easily.
10. My best days are still ahead of me.

Or write your own Hot Thought here:

_____

_____

STEP 2

"I"

INFLICT DAMAGE

7

SPEAK ONLY
WHAT YOU SEEK

It is not enough to have a good mind.
The main thing is to use it well.

—RENÉ DESCARTES

W E'VE ESTABLISHED THE IMPORTANCE of focusing on God and His ability rather than our failings. If you're anything like me, you are probably thinking this is easier said than done. Admittedly, it can be difficult to control your thoughts. In this Step you are going to learn how you can start programming your mind by first disciplining your mouth.

When you learn to consistently speak faith-filled words, you will accelerate your progress, elevate your mood, and effortlessly build confidence.

When you learn to consistently speak faith-filled words, you will accelerate your progress, elevate your mood, and effortlessly build confidence.

How do you do that? There's one simple rule: *Speak only what you seek.*

SNAKES ON A PLANE

The first time I learned about the power of words, I was on an airplane. We had begun to undergo severe turbulence. This wasn't your average run-of-the mill "wind pocket" we were experiencing; this was roller-coaster-action, hit-your-head-on-the-overhead-compartment stuff.

I gripped the passenger next to me, a pitiable business-man. I could feel my nails digging into his pale, innocent skin. I didn't even know his name. I didn't care.

In the past, this "carnival joy ride" at 40,000 feet would

have sent me into instant anxiety attack. However, luckily for the businessman, I had just been listening to a sermon on "the power of words."

The speaker explained in his message that, rather than *giving in* to fear, we should speak to it, and it would dissipate. He explained that we must dominate our negative thoughts and bring them into subjection to God. According to Scripture, "we take every thought captive to obey Christ."[22]

He went on to explain that the primary way we "can take captive our thoughts" is by speaking God's Word, and that when spoken, God's Word triumphantly overcomes fear. Furthermore, he taught that God's word is an "indispensable weapon."[23]

As the plane jerked right and my ice water spilled on the tray in front of me, I was skeptical at best. Straining to listen, my palms were sweating, and my heartbeat was thundering louder than the plane engine.

I began to speak: *"God has not given me a spirit of fear, but of love, power, and a sound mind"*[24] and *"Perfect love casts out all fear ..."*[25]

The strangest phenomenon occurred. The death-grip I had on my seating companion loosened. My breathing slowed. Almost, *almost*—a sensation of peace rippled down to my toes.

I was taken aback at the lessening of my symptoms. I began to feel something I hadn't felt in twenty years: hope. It was as if the world had turned brand-new. Suddenly, I didn't have to live life reactively. I could move against fear pro-actively.

I was speaking what I was seeking.

Deep within my belly, it was as if an "inner-superwoman" began to arise. Right in my plane seat, a war was raging deep within the recesses of my soul, with victory suspended in the balance.

Who would triumph? I had no idea! I just didn't want to wind up with my face in a bag.

All around me, people let out small cries, and passengers used their sick bags. The turbulence was so virulent, waves of fear swept throughout the cabin. Eventually the plane landed, and passengers slowly, tentatively, grabbed their belongings in a daze of exhaustion.

They walked toward the bright opening of the airplane door in a posture of sheer survival, hurling disgust at the attendants while disembarking. I arose and walked down the narrow aisle. In my step was energy, ecstasy, and the sense that I had just seen another miracle.

This was my first time.

This was my first flight.

I had not had an anxiety attack.

I had fought FEAR—and won.

During that plane ride it was as if I was introduced to a new person. Beneath the layers of fearful insecurity I had *thought* was me, lay hidden a different girl, a sort of wild girl, a girl unafraid to meet her Enemy. This was an inner "Wonder Woman" I had not met before!

It was the real me. Pleased to meet you, wild girl—killer boots!

WORDS HAVE CREATIVE POWER

Your words are a creative force. In the same way the Holy Spirit "hovered" over the deep waters in Genesis (1:2), your words are hovering over your life, inhibiting, or releasing your potential.

> Your words are a creative force hovering over your life, inhibiting, or releasing your potential.

You must learn to harness the creative power that's just *below your nose.*

Dr. Andrew Newberg and Mark Robert Waldman write in *Words Can Change Your Brain* that any form of negative rumination—for example, worrying about your health—will stimulate the release of destructive neurochemicals:

> *"In fact if I were to put you into an MRI scanner—a huge donut-shaped magnet that can take a video of the neural changes happening in your brain—and flash the word "NO" for less than one second, you'd see a sudden release of dozens of stress-producing hormones and neurotransmitters. These chemicals immediately interrupt the normal functioning of your brain, impairing logic, reason, language processing, and communication."*[26]

Vocalizing negativity releases stress chemicals not only in your brain, but in anyone else who is listening as well.

Additionally, a study published in the medical journal, *Neuroimage,* discovered that if you went one step further to *vocalize* your negativity, or even slightly frown when you say no, more stress chemicals will be released, not only in your brain, but in anyone else who is listening as well.[27]

Words have always had this kind of raw, creative power. We see the emphasis on the creative power of our words in the Bible through the repetition of the phrase "and God said" over 10 times in the narrative of Creation.[28] Notice the order of events. God **said,** and then He **saw.** He had an internal image, spoke it, and then physically it came to pass.

The Scriptures describe God as one who "**speaks** of the nonexistent things as if they already existed."[29] In addition, we are told that God made mankind in his likeness.[30] Thus, you are designed to create in the manner God did, by *unleashing containers of creative power, your words.*

The Rabbinic understanding of Genesis 2:7 further suggests your primary purpose, saying you are a "speaking spirit":

> *"And the Lord God created man in two formations; and took dust from the place of the house of the sanctuary, and from the four winds of the world, and mixed from all the waters of the world, and created him red, black, and white; and breathed into his nostrils the inspiration of life, and there was in the body of Adam the inspiration of a speaking spirit, unto the illumination of the eyes and the hearing of the ears."*[31]

In fact, the word "abracadabra"is actually from the Aramaic phrase, *avra kehdabra,* which literally translates, "I will *create* as I speak."

Your words are more powerful than you know.

SAY WHAT CAN BE, NOT WHAT IS

In the 1990s, a fascinating study was performed by Dr. Masaru Emoto where he studied the effect of words on the crystalline structure of water. He studied the shapes water would make, after both positive and negative words were spoken to it. The water was frozen and then studied under a dark field microscope.

In the water that was spoken positively to, the results showed gorgeous crystalline structures. Picture Elsa's sparkling ice castle in *Frozen.* In the water that was spoken negatively to, unattractive, disorderly, ugly shapes formed.

When one considers our bodies are made up of 70% water (in infants it is 90%), the ramifications for how our physical makeup is affected by words are astounding. Words are radically affecting your physical matter.

This is why it is critical you speak only what you seek, not continually describing what already is.

Jesus said it best when he said, "Truly I tell you, whoever

says to this mountain, 'Be lifted up and thrown into the sea!' And does not doubt in his heart but believes that what **he says** will take place, it will be done for him."[32]

One version of the Scripture states it like this: "He shall HAVE, whatever he SAYS."[33]

It's interesting that the word "says" occurs two times in the verse of Mark 11:23, and only one time do we see the word "believe." It's as if *believing* is important, but *saying* will actually bring something to pass.

There is just one problem.

Rather than having the good things we want, we settle for what we already have, by SAYING:

- "I can't seem to kick sugar."
- "I never drink enough water."
- "I can't seem to kick snacking before bed."
- "I HATE going to the gym."
- "I am SO not a morning person."
- "I'm just so disorganized!"
- "I'm just not disciplined like you."

Brian Tracy said, "Never say anything about yourself you do not want to come true." The declarations you are making about your health and wellness are coming to pass, whether good or bad.

Release the creative potential in your voice. Become brave in your body by releasing brave words. To begin seeing change, stop talking to God *about* how big your problems are, and start talking to your *problems* about how big your God is!

In my case, I wasn't saying many negative things regarding my body, I was thinking them. I was simply silent.

I wasn't speaking what I was seeking,
so I wasn't creating anything.

I wasn't speaking what I was seeking, so I wasn't creating anything.

Creative words have potential to change your situation. If you are not speaking anything **good**, then nothing **good** is being created.

As Elie Wiesel, the famous writer and noted Holocaust survivor said, *"Neutrality helps the oppressor, never the victim. Silence encourages the tormentor, never the tormented."*

Whether you are in a habit of saying bad things about yourself or you just don't know *what to say,* the next chapter is for you. Let's discover how you can go on the offensive, inflict damage, and become insanely brave through the power of speaking faith-filled words!

8

DEVELOP A BRAVE VOCABULARY

She looked so irresistibly beautiful as she said
those brave words that no man alive could
have steel his heart against her.

—WILKIE COLLINS, The Woman in White

OUR WORDS ARE SO POWERFUL that God has ordained that through speaking faith-filled words, we even pass from death to life. In the Christian faith, the verse in Romans 10:10 is one we view as "praying the prayer of salvation." While on face value, this text is about eternal life after death, there is a deeper meaning as well.

Take a look at Romans 10:10, *"For with the **heart** a person believes ... and with the **mouth** he confesses and confirms [his] salvation."*

When you study the word "salvation" in the Greek, *sōtēria,* you find this word speaks of our physical healing, as well as eternal life.

Another translation says, *"With the mouth confession **is made unto** salvation (healing)."*[34] The Scripture affirms that your words are the mechanism that confirms and establishes your health.

If the greatest miracle—salvation from eternal death—comes from the words of your mouth, how much more easily will your words renew your energy, vitality, and wellness as well?

DECLARE WHO YOU ARE!

In addition to bringing manifestation of your health, we also see how the Enemy flees at the power of God's Word in your mouth. Around 2,000 years ago, Satan was trying to trash-talk Jesus in the desert. Jesus, knowing the power of speaking faith-filled words, responded with the best kind of retort, *"It is written."*[35]

The Enemy, taunting him, came against Jesus's core identity, saying, "IF you are the son of God ..." In the same way, the Enemy wants to come against your God-given identity as a royal son or daughter of the Most-High.

He wants to trick you into believing that you *can't do it*, you don't have *what it takes*, you will never lose the weight, and you will NEVER become brave in your body.

My exhortation?

Don't believe him. HE'S A LIAR.

Rather, open your mouth as loud as you can and respond: "IT IS WRITTEN ..."

Only when you become VOCAL
do you become victorious.

Only when you become VOCAL do you become victorious. You will inflict damage to the dark, hidden places the Enemy has tormented you in when you speak God's Word out in faith. Rather than being the one *afflicted*, you will inflict damage to the Enemy with every faith-filled word.

James exhorts us, "Yell a loud no to the devil and watch him scamper."[36] As you verbalize your identity, watch the Devil flee, just like he did from Jesus!

Check out the following list of who God says you are, begin declaring who you are, and see true salvation, *sōtēria*, enter your situation today.

WHO YOU ARE IN CHRIST

- I am extraordinarily, greatly loved by God (Romans 1:7; Ephesians 2:4; Colossians 3:12; 1 Thessalonians 1:4).

- I am far from oppression, and fear does not come near me (Isaiah 54:14).

- I have the mind of Christ (1 Corinthians 2:16; Philippians 2:5).

- I have the peace of God that passes all understanding (Philippians 4:7).

- I have the Greater One living in me; greater is He Who is in me than he who is in the world (1 John 4:4).

- I have received the gift of righteousness and reign as a king in life by Jesus Christ (Romans 5:17).

- I have no lack, for my God supplies all of my needs according to His riches in glory by Christ Jesus (Philippians 4:19).

- I can do all things through Christ Jesus (Philippians 4:13).

- I am God's workmanship, created in Christ unto good works (Ephesians 2:10).

- I am a new creature in Christ (2 Corinthians 5:17).

- I am a joint-heir with Christ (Romans 8:17).

- I am more than a conqueror through Him Who loves me (Romans 8:37).

- I am an overcomer by the blood of the Lamb and the word of my testimony (Revelation 12:11).

- I am a partaker of His divine nature (2 Peter 1:3-4).

- I am the righteousness of God in Jesus Christ (2 Corinthians 5:21).

- I am the temple of the Holy Spirit; I am not my own (1 Corinthians 6:19).

- I am the head and not the tail; I am above only and not beneath (Deuteronomy 28:13).

- I am redeemed from the curse of sin, sickness, and poverty (Deuteronomy 28:15-68; Galatians 3:13).

- I am healed by the stripes of Jesus (Isaiah 53:5; 1 Peter 2:24).

- I am raised up with Christ and seated in heavenly places (Ephesians 2:6; Colossians 2:12).

- I am strengthened with all might according to His glorious power (Colossians 1:11).

- I am submitted to God, and the devil flees from me because I resist him in the Name of Jesus (James 4:7).

- For God has not given me a spirit of fear but of power, love, and a sound mind (2 Timothy 1:7).

To download a poster of these scriptures, just check out the resources at www.bravebodymethod.com.

Remember, as long as you are speaking good things according to God's Word, the Devil is losing!

Don't talk the problem, declare the promise.

Don't talk the problem, declare the promise.

The point is this: Successful people are geniuses at creating exciting pictures of the future through their words. To achieve a Brave Body, we have to begin to paint with our words, big, exciting pictures of our future.

It takes BRAVERY to believe there's a greater reality than what you might feel.

It takes bravery to speak truth in the face of a lie.

Stop speaking about your failures, and drop passing references to your mistakes and failures.

It takes bravery to speak truth
in the face of a lie. Stop speaking about your
failures, and drop passing references to
your mistakes and failures.

Cease negative self-talk and self-deprecating remarks. Speak as if you have *already* crossed the chasm. Speak only what you seek and inflict damage on the darkness.

In the next chapter, we are going to learn about how *seeing* what you are speaking will dramatically propel your weight loss goals, accelerate your self-acceptance, and give you that explosive vision that will cause you to bounce out of bed in the morning!

STEP 2 FUN SHEETS

What do you tend to do more — speak out negative remarks regarding yourself, or be quiet and just think them?

_____

_____

_____

Have you ever faced incredible fear like Eileen did on the airplane? What would it look like for you to move from being the one "afflicted," to being the one to "inflict damage" and declare out loud God's promises? How would you feel?

_____

_____

_____

What sort of things would you like to speak into existence regarding your health, confidence or appearance?

_____

_____

_____

Which verse resonates with you the most from the Scripture list (page 92)? Which one could you most imagine speaking out loud?

_____

_____

_____

To download a free poster of these scriptures, please visit
www.bravebodymethod.com.

STEP 3

"S"

SEE THE
GOD-PAINTING

9

Vision Board For Your Soul

I shut my eyes in order to see.

—PAUL GAUGIN

BECOMING MISS AMERICA was Tara Holland's only dream. She stepped out timidly and entered the Miss Florida pageant and won the title of first runner-up. She decided to enter again the following year, but once again she fell just short of the coveted first place crown. After moving to Kansas in 1997, she entered the Miss Kansas pageant and won the title.

That same year, she saw her dream come to pass when she went on to be crowned Miss America.

After the pageant, a reporter asked Tara the secret to her success. She admitted that she was tempted to give up having lost twice at the state-level competitions but instead became more committed to her goal. She went out and rented dozens of pageant videos, anything she could find—local, state, Miss Teen, Miss Universe.

She watched them over and over again.

She would pretend it was her in that situation. She pictured herself, head held high, walking the runway. She imagined hearing her name announced and the crown being placed on her head. Over and over, she envisioned herself succeeding.

The secret, Tara explained, was that she imagined herself winning *before it happened.*

"Were you nervous walking down the runway, in front of millions of people watching via television, as they played the Miss America song," inquired a reporter?

"No, I wasn't nervous at all," she replied. "You see, I had walked down that runway thousands of times before."[37]

Visualizing the plan God has for you is the third and vital step to achieving your Brave Body. For it's only when you see the exciting picture of your future, that you can incubate the promise and give birth to the results.

In this chapter we're going to learn about the secret

power of Biblical meditation and how it will expedite your progress, keep you motivated, and help you effortlessly lose weight.

AN EXCITING PICTURE OF THE FUTURE

If you're not seeing, you're most likely struggling.

> *Where there is no vision, the people perish.*
> —Proverbs 29:18 KJV

Unnecessary suffering comes when you don't have an exciting picture before your eyes.

Unnecessary suffering comes when you don't have an *exciting* picture before your eyes.

The word "perish" actually means "die."

When you don't have vision, you are actually dying while you are alive. You notice there is **no joy,** no spark, no *hope* that anything could change. As the author Victor Hugo said, "When a man is out of sight, it is not too long before he is out of mind."

However, the good news is that when you uncover the unbelievably exciting, blood-pumping, mind-blowing vision God has for your life, you will discover limitless energy, momentum, and motivation you didn't even know you possessed! THEN the more you move toward it, you will experience accelerated progress due to the law of sowing and reaping. The power of vision is unbelievable.

As you locate the vision and purpose God has for you, you will literally begin to bounce out of bed in the morning. Olympic athletes, performers, and businessman have been employing this Biblical truth for centuries.

I read where famous hotelier Conrad Hilton, upon seeing a photograph of the grandeur of the Waldorf Astoria hotel in New York City, decided he would make it his goal to one day own that hotel. He printed out the picture and slid it below the glass in his office desk.

Eighteen years later, when he bought 250,000 shares of the property, he did indeed become the owner. His dream became a reality. The photograph served as a vision, an exciting picture of his future, for him to incubate into reality.

"Do not let [my words] out of your sight."
—Proverbs 4:21

In the book of Proverbs, we are exhorted, *"Do not let [my words] out of your **sight**."*[38]

It's only when we keep the **exciting vision of health that God desires for us** before our eyes that we begin to see results. In fact, having this exciting picture has proven so effective at achieving results it can even cause improvement without your doing a thing.

In an experiment, Dr. Alan Richardson divided basketball players into 3 groups and tested each player's ability to make free throws. They were instructed as follows:

- 1st Group: Practice free throws 20 minutes every day.
- 2nd Group: Visualize yourself shooting perfect baskets.
- 3rd Group: Do not practice or visualize.

- 1st Group: Who practiced—improved 24%
- 2nd Group: Who *visualized*—improved an astonishing 23%

The results were astounding:

- 1st Group: Who practiced—improved 24%.
- 2nd Group: Who *visualized—improved an astonishing 23%.*
- 3rd Group: Who did nothing—experienced no improvement.[39]

The group that *only visualized* experienced significant improvement, almost *as much as the guys who actually practiced.*

Through visualizing and dreaming,
you can incubate the promises of God
and give birth to the results.

Through visualizing and dreaming, you can incubate the promises of God and give birth to the results!

As Albert Einstein said, "Our imagination is just a preview of life's coming attractions." Let me ask you a question: What is your imagination showing you?

Have you ever walked down the runway? Have
you ever seen yourself in your best body?
Have you ever witnessed that picture of
yourself being bold, brave, and beautiful?

Have you ever walked down the runway? Have you ever seen yourself in your best body? Have you ever witnessed that picture of yourself being bold, brave, and beautiful?

Do you keep that vision of victory in front of you?

Tara Holland knew she would never be a winner until she first saw herself as a winner. She had to replace the vision of herself as "Miss Runner-up" with "Miss America."

Conrad Hilton had to visualize himself owning the Waldorf-Astoria before he owned it in reality. Athletes advanced their playing ability solely by imagining themselves making free throws.

You need to see yourself in your Brave Body—healthy and energetic—before you will see it physically. Get an exciting picture of who you really can become!

Now let's look at how God used visualization in the Bible and how glimpsing the God-Painting for your life will bring about maximum success.

10

THE GOD-PAINTING WILL TAKE YOUR BREATH AWAY

I will meditate on Your precepts,
and contemplate Your ways.
—PSALM 119:15 NKJV

W ALT DISNEY DIED BEFORE DISNEY WORLD in Florida could be completed. On opening day in 1971, almost five years after his death, someone commented to Mike Vance, creative director of Walt Disney Studios, *"Isn't it too bad Walt Disney didn't live to see this?"*

"He did see it," Vance replied simply. *"That's why it's here."*[40]

When God wanted to plant the vision in Abraham's heart, he took him out to the night sky and said, "Look up at the sky and count the stars."[41] Scientists say that with the human eye, we can count 6,000 stars. The Father said, "Your children are going to become as numerous as all these stars."

I imagine that when Abraham heard those words, he felt his heart burn. He was probably swept up with emotion, imagining the legacy he would leave on the earth. As a man without children, in a culture that viewed sons as the greatest asset, it was probably difficult to grasp the depth of these words.

I imagine his eyes welled up with tears, and his clear view of each star became a shimmering wash of hope.

I bet he didn't go to sleep that night. Or if he did, perhaps the echoes of "Daddy!" and the pitter-patter of little feet ran through his mind.

God used the language of dreams and visions because He wanted Abraham to see with the eyes of his heart. God needed Abraham to **incubate it on the inside,** before he could see with his natural eyes.

It didn't take long with those dreams and visions, incubating in that 100-year old body.

Soon he had transformed into a youthful, rejuvenated body, capable of fathering his first child. It must have rubbed off on Sarah too! Later in the story, 92-year-old Sarah was so attractive that King Abimelech tried to take her as his own wife!

The Bible mentions "meditate" or "meditation" over 20 times.

Meditation is a powerful theme in the Bible. The Bible mentions "meditate" or "meditation" over 20 times. In fact, the Bible commands us to meditate. In Joshua 1:8, God says to meditate on His word day and night so we will obey it. The psalmist says, "his delight is in the law of the Lord, and in His law he meditates day and night."[42]

Meditation is focused thinking.
It takes serious effort. You select a verse and reflect on it over and over in your mind …
if you know how to worry, you already know how to meditate.

Rick Warren, in *The Purpose Driven Life*, describes meditation this way: "Meditation is *focused thinking*. It takes serious effort. You select a verse and reflect on it over and over in your mind … if you know how to worry, you already know how to meditate."[43]

We are, in fact, meditating all the time. Most of the time we meditate on what's going to go wrong, how we'll never succeed, or how people don't like us—or in my case, all of those things at one time! I was implementing the kind of meditation author Seth Godin describes in this way: "Anxiety is practicing failure in advance."

Rick Warren went on to say, "No other habit can do more to transform your life and make you more like Jesus than daily reflection on Scripture … If you look up all the times God speaks about meditation in the Bible, you will be amazed at the benefits He has promised to those who take the time to reflect on His Word throughout the day."[44]

BIBLICAL MEDITATION IS VISUAL

So how can we demystify meditation and apply it to our everyday lives, so that we can experience the fullest measure of God's Painting?

Firstly, we must recognize that there is an unseen realm from which everything we see with our eyes was created. Everything we see was once an idea in the mind of its creator. The essence of meditation is this:

We see before we do.

Jesus said it best when he declared, "the Son can do nothing by himself; he can do only what he sees his Father doing."[45] What a picture of true success—meditating and then doing only what the Father shows us.

I love how God intrinsically ties meditation to our success in life:

Do not let this Book of the Law depart from your mouth,
*but you shall **meditate** on it day and night,*
so that you may be careful to do everything written in it.
Then you will be prosperous and successful.
—Joshua 1:8 NIV

The Hebrew word for meditate in this passage is *hagah* which means "to meditate, imagine, visualize, mutter."[46]

*Meditate on it **[visually and verbally imagine it]** day and night ... Then you will be prosperous and successful.*

When the Bible talks about **meditating on the Word,** it refers to dwelling continually in a manner that's *seen* and *heard.*

When the Bible talks about meditating in the Word, it refers to dwelling continually in a manner that's *seen* and *heard*.

Dr. David Yonggi Cho, who pastors the largest church in the world, in his book, *The Fourth Dimension,* suggests a daily ritual of visualization in the mornings following prayer to achieve maximum success.[47]

True Biblical Meditation means making God's promise so real on the inside, it's **only a matter of time** before you see it on the outside. Much like a pregnant woman, the Word can grow inside of us and become so real that it's only a matter of time till we are holding the promise in our arms.

YOU ARE MOVING TOWARDS WHAT YOU ARE *SEEING*

There was a man in the Bible named Jacob, whose name meant "the swindler." He worked hard for his uncle, Laban, for over twenty years. They had a contentious relationship, in which they frequently deceived each other.

Jacob said, "Uncle, I'll work for you on one condition. You take away all the spotted and speckled animals from me, and I'll tend only the animals with coats of solid colors.

And if these solid-colored animals give birth to spotted and speckled offspring, then these will become my salary."

Thinking he got a great deal, Laban agreed. Laban removed the spotted and speckled animals, and Jacob was left with the animals of solid color. Jacob went to the mountain, and through a *dramatic* arts and crafts project, made a "vision board" of spots and speckles for his animals to look at every time they drank water.

What happened next is mind-boggling.

Soon, all these animals gave birth to spotted and speckled offspring!

The calves that were a solid color gave birth to speckled offspring, as a result of what they held before their eyes daily.

This demonstrates the powerful principle that **we are always moving in the direction of what we see.**

> Your are moving right now in
> the direction of what you see.

LOSING WEIGHT BY THE POWER OF MEDITATION

Recent research conducted by Consumer Reports and the American Psychological Association showed how meditation and mindfulness training was considered an "excellent" or "good" strategy for weight loss by seven out of 10 psychologists in their survey.[48]

Quite literally, sustained meditation leads to something called neuroplasticity, which is defined as the brain's ability to change, structurally and functionally, on the basis of environmental input.

For much of the last century, scientists believed that the brain essentially stopped changing after adulthood.

But research by University of Wisconsin neuroscientist Richard Davidson showed that practicing meditation causes high levels of gamma wave activity. Put simply, they're automatically able to control their thoughts and reactiveness.[49]

I had no idea how powerful meditation was until I was in college and fully immersed in a binge-eating disorder. In this particular season, I was waking up in the middle of the night and experiencing an uncontrollable urge to eat vast amounts of food.

I felt completely out of control.

I was overweight and had lost my monthly cycle due to the damage I was doing to my body. I remember the pain in my heart, the exhaustion from constant self-loathing, and the mental torment from obsessing over every bite I put in my mouth.

I was disordered in my eating,
because I was disordered in my soul.

I was alive but experiencing *death*.

I was disordered in my eating, because I was **disordered** in my soul. Around that time, a Scripture seemed to JUMP out at me:

> *The things which are impossible with men, are possible with God.* —Luke 18:27 KJV

Healing seemed impossible.

Losing weight seemed impossible.

Coming out from under a cloud of depression seemed impossible.

But in that place of "impossible," I sensed the Holy Spirit whisper to me: *Close your eyes.*

I can only describe what happened next as a dance between my mind and Heaven. I had a picture of *me*, smiling, thin, and truly, truly healthy and beautiful. My heart **leapt inside of me** as the power of this picture washed over me.

It was the first time I could remember feeling hope in a long, long time.

God was speaking—For the things that are impossible with YOU, Eileen, ARE possible with Me.

It was as if this picture, this "God-Painting" of the future, became a possibility. It was clear I couldn't make it happen, but that God would make it happen.

And a funny thing occurred—I felt I had **faith** for the very first time.

The Book of Hebrews teaches that "faith is the substance of things hoped for."[50]

"Substance" in the Greek language is *hypostasis*. In the English language this can be translated as "title deed or legal paper." As I opened my eyes, I felt that I had somehow been given this title deed. Somehow, it was "mine" in the unseen realm.

I felt the Lord tell me to open my eyes and write on a piece of paper a number. In my heart, I knew it was the weight He wanted me to be.

To be honest, the weight I wrote down was less than I ever remembered weighing before. I was timid and unsure in my mind, but in my heart I felt something different—*assurance.*

Since that time, I've learned that this "assurance" is something ushered in by the Holy Spirit. It is a rest. A peace in knowing that you have a promise from God on the inside. I imagine Abraham, gazing at the beautiful night sky, listening to the Creator paint for him this glorious destiny picture, felt this assurance.

When God divinely grants you this "title deed," whether you see those things, they are spiritually bound to come to you because they belong to you.

I wonder what God wants to show you in your heart?

God says we are transformed as we "look,"[51] and the Holy Spirit wants to fill your eyes with His dreams, visions, and images:

"In the last days, God says, I will pour out my Spirit on all people. Your sons and daughters will prophesy, your young men will see visions, your old men will dream dreams."
—Acts 2:17 NIV

People like to say, "Don't just sit there; do *something!*" I want to encourage you: **Don't** do something; just **SIT there.**

What energizing picture of the future is He giving you?

In the next chapter, we're going to break down the steps to discover how easy it is to see this picture, and the explosive potential it carries to thrust you into your dreams.

11

HOW TO SEE
THE GOD-PAINTING
IN 7 EASY STEPS

The courage to imagine the otherwise is our greatest resource,
adding color and suspense to all our life.

—DANIEL J. BOORSTIN

THERE WAS A FASCINATING STUDY conducted in 1979 in which Harvard MBA graduates were asked, "Have you set clear, written goals for your future and made plans to accomplish them?" The result—only 3% had written goals and plans, 13% had goals but they weren't in writing, and 84% had no goals at all.

Ten years later, the same group was interviewed again, and the result was absolutely mind-blowing! The 13% of the class who had goals but did not write them down was earning twice the amount of the 84% who had no goals.

The 3% who had written goals were earning, on average, ten times as much as the other 97% of the class!

While this study only looks at earnings to quantify success, I still find it to be an extremely motivating example of why creating clear and measurable goals and writing them down is a key to success.

Write the vision; make it plain on tablets, so he may run who reads it. —Habakkuk 2:2 ESV

Habakkuk 2:2 says, "Write the vision; make it plain on tablets, so he may run who reads it."[52] Writing down your vision is crucial for your success.

WHAT DO YOU WANT?

Now I'm going to ask you a question: *What do you really want?*

This question may terrify you. I totally get it. In our era of history, so many choices are available to us. Almost too many—it's overwhelming!

We can sympathize with mathematician-philosopher Blaise Pascal, when he said, "The eternal silence of these infinite spaces frightens me." However, it is crucial that you become specific regarding your desire.

- But what if I never lose the weight?
- What if I make a commitment and can't keep it?
- What if I don't know what I want?

Too often we get caught up in the "what ifs," and this hinders our progress: One key—start with your desires.

Clarity breeds power.

Jesus said it like this, "Whatsoever things you DESIRE when you ask them, believe you shall have them, and you shall receive them."[53] When you get specific about *what you want,* that's when God can answer. Clarity breeds power.

The first step in creating a God-Painting is to start thinking about these three questions. Close your eyes and peer into the future.[54]

What does your body ideally look like?

What else do you see and feel that lets you realize you have achieved success?

Don't worry about **how** you're going to achieve it. Over the next 21 days, just focus on describing what you see.

One helpful exercise is to imagine that you're filming every aspect of your life: your appearance, your activities, your projects, your eating routine, your fitness routine, etc. Imagine that what the Bible says is true and apply it to your situation.

- Think of your ideal health as *already* existing.
- Picture yourself strong and confidently moving through the situation.[55]
- Picture yourself full of peace as you awaken.[56]
- Picture yourself disciplined in that routine.[57]

Work to develop a clear picture that is visual and specific with regards to your emotional health, weight, figure shape, energy levels, style, and state of being. Play the film in your mind. What do the big picture and the details of your life look like 21 days from now?

Here are a few steps to get you started on the right path. Begin recording what you see here, but don't stop! Finish what you see in your own personal journal.

These could be some of the most important thoughts you will ever write!

HOW TO SEE YOUR GOD-PAINTING

Make sure laptops are off and phones are disabled.
It's important your mind isn't distracted.

1. Find A Sacred Space.
While all of us would love to take a 3-day trip to the Bahamas, the reality is this might not happen. Endeavor to find a peaceful space. Get in a relaxed position, perhaps reclined or lying down (but not where you might fall asleep!).

2. Become Quiet And/Or Put On Instrumental Music.
Still your mind by putting on relaxing music without words, so that other, unintended mental images don't pop up! I have found some wonderful instrumental albums that you can find links to on my site, www.bravebodymethod.com.

3. Focus Your Attention Upon The Word.
Open your Bible or the list of *Who You Are in Christ* scriptures on page 92, and begin saying them out loud, or finding just one that seems to speak to you.

Invite the Holy Spirit into your time by praying a simple prayer such as:

Lord, I dedicate this time to You.
Will you speak to me now with dreams and visions?
Give me a clear picture of how you see me
and what You desire in the areas of my wellness.

4. Don't Ask, "How?" Ask, "What?"

Don't be surprised if the Holy Spirit starts illuminating your mind or prodding you with exciting pictures of your future. He may prompt you with questions like "What do you want?" or "How do *you* want to look?" or you can ask Him. There's no formula.

Remember, don't get caught up in HOW it will happen; stay in the vein of WHAT will happen.

Make a mental note of what you are seeing. *Be specific: What are you wearing? How do you feel?*

Did the Holy Spirit reveal an ideal weight for you? Or do you envision the weight you believe the Holy Spirit desires for you?

5. Keep At It Until You Get A Feeling Of Calm And Confidence.

If you aren't getting a vibrant or exciting picture, don't worry! Set the exercise down and come back to it in a day. God speaks to all of us differently, so be prepared for a custom tailored image and experience all your own.

Like Rick Warren said, meditation is "focused thinking" and takes dedication and persistence. But the rewards are unmatched!

I encourage you to adapt this practice into your daily routine—and watch in amazement at how God will begin showing up in surprising ways.

6. Emerge With A Smile.

I love how Coach Tommy Newberry says, "Arise from prayer each time with a jubilant smile overtaking your face!" This posture is such an act of faith in the goodness of God and how He is "for you, not against you."[58] Emerge with a smile!

"Arise from prayer each time with a jubilant smile overtaking your face!" —Tommy Newberry

---

7. Add Pictures To Your God-Painting.

To stimulate your imagination, go the extra mile and add images, photographs, and designs that inspire and captivate your spirit. I attach physical images to my vision, such as a photo of myself at my ideal weight and images of fitness and health. I keep these images in front of my eyes daily.

I've even downloaded an app to my phone (find suggestions at www.bravebodymethod.com), which keeps it mobile when I'm on the go. I love praying over my vision every day, thanking God that my dreams and goals regarding my health and other areas are coming to pass!

Just like Jacob's calves, your life is moving in the direction of what you hold before your eyes! Look for the *Fun Sheets* at the end of the book to practice this vital exercise every day.

Admittedly, simply visualizing your end goal is not going to get you there. Once you begin meditating, speaking, and seeing, the next step is to "Start Before You're Ready" through small, but powerful actions.

To find additional suggestions for your God-Painting,
please visit www.bravebodymethod.com.

In the next chapter we are going to learn how incremental, consistent action done in a spirit of faith can bring the results you've been dreaming for.

STEP 3 FUN SHEETS

When you don't have vision, you are actually dying while you are alive. You notice there is no joy, no spark, no hope that anything could change." Is this statement something you can relate to? Have you ever felt stuck by not having a clear vision?

_____

_____

_____

Carve out some time this next week to See Your God Painting:

1. Find a sacred space.

2. Become quiet and/or put on instrumental music.

3. Focus your attention upon the word.

4. Don't ask "how?" Ask "what?"

5. Keep at it until you get a feeling of calm and confidence.

6. Emerge with a smile.

7. Add pictures to your god-painting.

What energizing picture of the future is God giving you? Record some of what you see here. (Be specific: What are you wearing? How do you feel? Use present tense.)

_____

_____

_____

In the future when you have achieved your ideal body and ideal life ... what does it look like? What do you see and feel, or hear from people, that lets you realize you have achieved success?

_____

_____

_____

Did the Holy Spirit reveal an ideal weight for you? (Optional)

_____

_____

_____

The weight I believe You desire for me is: _____

131

STEP 4

"S"

START BEFORE YOU ARE READY

12

ACT AS IF

Vision without execution is hallucination.
—THOMAS EDISON

T HROUGHOUT HUMAN HISTORY, it's always been those men and women who plan and take consistent, persistent *action* who accomplish their goals. As you partake in quick, decisive action, your confidence in God and in yourself is going to skyrocket!

When God offered the Torah to the children of Israel, they did not say, "Let us hear what God wants, and then we'll do it."

Instead they responded in what seems to be the wrong order: *"We will do* and we will hear."[59]

"We will do and we will hear." —The Israelites

Unmistakable clarity and closeness to God occur when you begin putting action to your faith.

SOW THE SEED OF ACTION

As you begin taking "mini-steps," you are going to feel an incredible closeness to God. It will feel as if you are right in the center of His will and smack in the middle of His timing.

You will lose that sense of "I'm moving too slow, I should be so much further than I am now" because you will feel the Holy Spirit's pleasure all over you.

"Thinking won't overcome fear,
but action will." —W. Clement Stone

W. Clement Stone said, "Thinking won't overcome fear, but action will." Want to defeat fear? Action is the key.

When you take quick decisive action, your confidence will rise, your security will return, and a sense of boundless adventure will be released. In the words of Thomas Jefferson, "Do you want to know who you are? Don't ask. Act! Action will delineate or define you."

> "Do you want to know who you are?
> Don't ask. Act! Action will delineate or
> define you." —Thomas Jefferson

ACT AS IF

Too often we wait to "feel it" before we "do it."

In God's Kingdom, action is an expression of faith. Taking that initial step is subject to our will, but faith-filled action opens the door for the miraculous.

Unbelievable power from God will flood your world as you take Him at his Word and begin acting as if you are, right now, the confident, worthy, royal Son or Daughter of the Most High.

> You are brave when you stop hiding and begin
> acting like God's Word is true,
> even when you don't feel like it.

You are brave when you stop hiding and begin acting like God's Word is true, even when you don't feel like it.

As William Shakespeare wrote, "Assume the attitude, though you have it not." It's only when we **start acting as if God's Word is true,** that we can plan for success. We become energized, activated, and alive to exciting possibilities!

THE LAW OF THE SEED

A common misconception is that action always has to be BIG. The truth is, it's always been the opposite—small actions yield HUGE results.

In *The 4-Hour Body,* Tim Ferriss uses the concept of the "minimum effective dose" (MED). He defines it as "the smallest dose that will produce the desired outcome ... anything beyond the MED is wasteful."[60]

Boiled water is boiled water. Higher temperatures won't make it *more* boiled!

In fact, the Bible gives us an illustration of power in a tiny form of nature: a seed. Here is the Law of the Seed in action:

> *Do not be deceived, God is not mocked,*
> *for whatever a man sows, this he will also reap.*
> *For the one who sows to his own flesh*
> *shall from the flesh reap corruption,*
> *but the one who sows to the Spirit*
> *shall from the Spirit reap eternal life.*
> —Galatians 6:7–8 ESV

Many times we begin by trying to move a giant tree when God is only asking us to plant a seed.

Do what you can; God will do what you cannot.

There are over 42 references to "seeds"
in the New Testament.

There are over 42 references to "seeds" in the New Testament, and Jesus uses this metaphor frequently to describe how the Kingdom of God operates. To understand this concept fully, we must examine how vital "seeds and sowing" are in the Bible.

When you understand that every action and thought you have **is a seed you are *sowing*,** you will then have the power to change the RESULT. For years, you have sown seeds unknowingly, not understanding that **everything** you choose is a seed—every thought, every word, every bite, every workout.

In fact, what we experience as our current reality, is merely the fruition of seeds that we've sown throughout our lives. Today's harvest was yesterday's seed come to bear.

While the earth remains, seedtime and harvest, and cold and heat, and summer and winter, and day and night shall not cease.
—Genesis 8:22 NASB

God is saying, "Here is my foundational principle and law within which I operate. You are sowing, and you are reaping. It will remain in force as long as the earth remains." According to the Scripture, seed-bearing fruit is a foundational principle we simply cannot get away from.

The law of seedtime and harvest cannot be violated.

"...He that sows to the Spirit shall of the Spirit reap life everlasting." —Galatians 6:8

Once we learn how to sow seeds of health, we will see our habits change rapidly and surprisingly. Paul writes in

Galatians, "For he who sows to his flesh will of the flesh reap corruption, but he who sows to the Spirit will of the Spirit reap everlasting life."

The Greek word for flesh, *sárks*, refers to making decisions and actions *according to self* (i.e., done *apart from faith*).

In short, *flesh* generally relates to *what you do relying on your human effort,* i.e., decisions (actions) apart from a heart-reliance upon the supernatural grace of God.[61]

> Sowing to the Spirit is when you perform an action, but your attitude is believing in God to supernaturally do what only He can do.

In contrast, sowing to the Spirit is when you perform an action, but your attitude is believing in God to supernaturally do what only He can do. You are acting from a place of authority knowing who you are in Christ and what the finished work of the cross has accomplished for you.

Your small seeds of action sown in FAITH yield powerful results!

All one woman had to do was *stretch out her hand,* and instantly she was healed.[62] As you sow seeds to the Spirit, trusting God, miracles can't help but show up!

MY FLESH HAD A FIT

When you begin sowing seeds of discipline and self-control, seeds to the Spirit, **don't be surprised if your body and emotions start having a fit.**

> When you begin sowing seeds of discipline and self-control—seeds to the Spirit— don't be surprised if your body and emotions start having a FIT.

During my years of disordered eating, I always ate before bedtime. When I learned the power of sowing to the spirit a seed of faith, I committed to sow "bedtime eating" to the Lord in faith for my breakthrough. I committed to 5 days at first.

I found that through advanced decision-making, I could brainstorm what I would do instead of bedtime eating. Through deciding ahead of time, I found my obedience was much more consistent. Instead of eating, I came up with three non-eating activities: writing in my journal, going for an evening walk, or reading with a hot tea.

At first, I thought I might die when it hit 9pm and I didn't give my body the cookies it craved. In fact, my flesh had a fit!

But soon, through choosing and writing down my non-eating activity ahead of time, I began seeing results in the form of self-control. This rolled over into greater discipline during my daytime eating as well. I would choose water over Diet Coke or grilled chicken instead of fried.

I even LEFT FOOD ON MY PLATE at restaurants. What???

I was ecstatic! I had a whole new lease on life. Sowing to the Spirit was incredible! When the Bible says you reap "eternal life," it is NOT joking.

Pretty soon, my pant size went down, and my confidence started growing.

As you too start experiencing the eternal life—of peace, wholeness, and self-control—you'll never look back. You just won't tolerate things you used to before.

Eventually, you'll have trouble remembering how bad it really was, and your disordered past will fade to memory.

Through the grace and power of God, you absolutely can change your body and have a life you love.

I thought all the years I had sowed to the flesh with uncontrolled eating would require huge action, but my healing process came through the power of a seed.

I thought all the years I had sowed to the flesh with un-controlled eating would require **huge** action, but my healing process came through the power of a seed.

You do the small thing He is asking, and you will harvest huge results. Sow your seed in an **attitude of trusting God** and his Word to enact spiritual victory on your behalf.

Your quick decisive action won't happen without a fight—in the next chapter you're going to discover there's a war over your seed and how to emerge victorious every time.

13

RESISTANCE: THE WAR IS OVER YOUR SEED OF ACTION

Don't dig up in doubt what you planted in faith.
—ELISABETH ELLIOT

AS WE SOW TO THE SPIRIT, we begin to dismantle the power the Enemy has taken in our life and in two words, crush him.

Be warned: *He will not like your action.*

Let's go back to the beginning, where God cursed the Enemy.

> *I will put enmity between you [the Enemy]*
> *and the woman, and between your seed*
> *and her seed; he shall bruise your head,*
> *and you shall bruise his heel.*
> —Genesis 3:15 RSV

We see the same pattern again in Revelation, where Satan again pursues the woman and her seed.[63] While the traditional understanding of these scriptures is that "seed" refers to the Messiah, I believe that Satan is also at war with the seeds of your faith-filled action.

SEED OF MY BODY

A number of years ago, my husband and I were desperately trying to have a baby. I would become pregnant, only to lose the baby about 6–8 weeks later. This happened three times. Finally I received the diagnosis of "recurrent miscarriage" by our health professionals.

We were devastated. "Maybe it's just not God's will for you to ever have children," someone said to me.

Perhaps it is true that God's plan does not necessarily include children for everyone. However, her words didn't sit right with *me*. There was something I couldn't shake. I sensed I was in the midst of a battle.

One day when I was crying out to God I felt Him speak to me: *The war is always over your seed.*

Suddenly I knew I had a word from God that we were to pursue having a baby, whatever it took. My doctor ran tests and discovered that I had Factor V Leiden, a genetic predisposition to blood clotting.

The treatment was to take a shot **in my abdomen** once a day.

A shot? In my stomach?! I don't know, Lord.

To say I hate needles is an understatement. I have not once, but multiple times, passed out at the **sight** of a needle. When the doctor said a daily shot was going to be the key to getting pregnant, I think I gasped.

I knew this was a Brave Body moment. Would I be willing to defeat the Enemy's pursuit of my seed? I decided that with every shot I took, I would sow it as a "seed of faith," trusting God for my healthy baby. Every time the shot went in, I would imagine dealing a blow to the Enemy.

It wasn't enough to know he was against my seed; I needed to respond in faith-filled action. In the same way, *you must sow a seed to meet your need.*

147

START BEFORE YOU ARE READY

It is critical that you commit your action to the
Lord, believing for supernatural results.

1. Sow in Faith

It is critical that you commit your action to the Lord,
believing for supernatural results. If you don't, it's just wast-
ed. Have the kind of tenacity that one woman in the Bible
did. She knew that if she could just sow a seed of touching
Jesus, her whole world would shift.[64]

Every time you take action, do it in the spirit of "God
can turn this whole thing around, and He's doing so—right
now."

2. Sow Your Best

Understand that because of what you're doing—sowing a
seed to God—you must sow your best seed in faith. Stirred
with heart-felt generosity, David proclaimed: "I will not
present burnt offerings that have cost me nothing!"[65]

In order to sow to the Spirit, and not the flesh, consider
what it would really "cost you" and sow that in faith.

If you decide to sow bedtime eating, make sure that it

isn't a normal, easy activity for you to give up. Or if you decide to sow drinking soda, make sure that's something you actually do and you know you'll feel it! If you haven't drunk soda in the last 6 months, this is not sowing your best seed.

3. Cultivate an Expectancy to See Results!

Whatever you sow, believe in seeing results, quickly. Keep your eyes out for weight to drop, for a newfound energy, for that spark of confidence to hit you. It may be that someone offers you an encouraging compliment, like:

"What have you been doing lately? You look amazing!"

It may be that you lose more pounds than you had thought that week.

It may be you that start craving kale—miracles happen!

Be assured, if you start sowing to the Spirit, the Bible says you are going to reap "life everlasting!" Don't miss a moment of it.

In the next chapter we are going to find out which three seeds to sow for maximum impact.

14

THREE SEEDS FOR
MAXIMUM RESULTS

Crying is for plain women,
Pretty women go shopping.
—OSCAR WILDE

DALE **CARNEGIE SAID,** *"If you want to conquer fear, don't sit home and think about it. Go out and get busy."* In my experience, there are three kinds of seeds you can sow that will produce maximum results in your journey: eating seeds, exercise seeds, and seeds of confidence.

There are three kinds of seeds you can sow to
maximize your results: eating seeds, exercise
seeds, and seeds of confidence.

All three of these working together begin to weave a tapestry of beautiful self-care and begin affirming the God-identity inside of you. Working concurrently, you will begin to feel better, look better, and gain a striking sense of order.

1. EATING SEEDS

For Americans, eating can be out of control in many ways. Preoccupation with fad diets, overeating, unbalanced nutrition, or even obsessing about what you ate long after you've finished!

Recognize that God desires to be involved with your eating, and He wants it to bring healing and wholeness to you. However, it's easy to get out of control, and we must sow a seed of self-control to reap self-control.

> *Who satisfies your mouth with good*
> *so that your youth, renewed, is like the eagle's*
> *[strong, overcoming, soaring]!*
> —Psalm 103:5

Purpose to sow an eating seed, like dinner, sweets, or bedtime eating, and offer it to God in faith for your total and complete healing. It's important to sow your best eating seed, one that is sacrificial.

For instance, if you tend to overeat when watching TV, then that's your best seed. If you are out of control when you are at a restaurant, that is your best seed. If you tend to never eat breakfast, your seed might be eating breakfast every morning.

For me, I was out of control at night, so that was sowing my best seed. I gave the time after 8pm to God and chose instead to read with hot tea, walk, or journal (one of those) every night for 21 days.

And every night, I would feel His comfort, pleasure, and grace to help me for those 21 days.

What do you love to do? Is it cleaning out an old closet, scrapbooking, sports-watching, baking?

Separate yourself to that special activity as an act of worship to your Creator.

Separate yourself to that special activity as an act of worship to your Creator.

I also love the Jewish practice known as *Taanis HaRaavad,* where they leave a little food on each plate before the last morsel is gone. They do this to show that they will not overindulge in food and as a sign of honor to the Creator.

Perhaps your seed might look like this!

Whatever you choose, I encourage you to find your best seed, sow it in FAITH—and watch how the enemy becomes defeated!

Pray this simple prayer over your eating seed (insert your own words):

> *Father, I sow _____ as a seed in faith.*
> *It's impossible with me, but thank you, it's possible with*
> *YOU to help me. Instead of _____, I decide ahead*
> *of time to _____(non-eating activity).*
> *Strengthen me in Jesus' Name. Amen.*

2. EXERCISE SEEDS

Find something you think is manageable, *even if it's 10 minutes,* and just start. Sow it as a seed in faith and watch for miraculous results!

When I discovered this principle, I began "sowing my best seed" of exercise three times a week. I would set my mind and sow my best seed of 10 minutes of cardio three times a week.

"Only ten minutes?" you ask.

Yep, 10 minutes. It was the best seed I had.

The key is simple: It isn't the type of program you are on, it's the seed sown in a spirit of faith as you do it unto God.

As I was faithful to sow my best, I found the extra weight I'd been carrying started coming off. The key is—**it isn't the type of program you are on,** it's the seed **sown in a spirit of faith** as you do it unto God.

Pray like this before you exercise:

> *God, you said I am the Temple of the Holy Spirit.*
>
> *Right now I sow this exercise seed in faith.*
> *It's impossible for me to lose all this weight,*
> *but with you NOTHING is impossible!*
> *I am overjoyed at how I know you are going to*
> *help me get through these 10 minutes!*

3. CONFIDENCE SEEDS

Too often we wait to "feel" like doing something before we take action. However, the opposite is true—you must *act your way into feeling.*

Dr. William James of Harvard put it this way, "Action seems to follow feelings, but really action and feelings go together; and by regulating the action which is under the more **direct control of the will,** we can indirectly regulate the feeling which is not."

What this is saying is you will "feel it"
once you begin acting it out.

What this is saying is you will "feel it" once you begin acting it out.

You can apply the "seed principle" in other areas as well. For years, I struggled with feeling shy and anxious when I got up in front of people. I wanted to run the other way! Sometimes I would become so nervous before getting up in front of people, I would be physically ill from the nerves. I thought I'd never be able to speak coherently in front of people. I felt like such a failure.

One time before singing at church, I actually just ran away! I threw the microphone to my husband, mumbled some sort of excuse, and went home. I was still learning this idea that though **I didn't feel like sowing a seed, I could do it on purpose, anyway.**

When I learned I could "sow a seed of faith" by simply *acting confident,* I was amazed at the results. I wasn't doing it for other people, but unto God—so even though my knees were shaky and my voice was dry, I'd just get up anyway. Soon, I'd relax and not be such a nervous wreck.

Emotions are temporary,
but God's word is eternal.

Emotions are ***temporary,*** but God's word is ***eternal.***

It will outlast your emotions any day. If you just hold on long enough, your emotions will quiet down and your spirit will take over.

By acting like the Word is true and you are who God says you are, you are sowing a powerful seed of confidence into your spirit. Soon, because you are acting in faith, confidence will begin to become normal.

I love how Joyce Meyer said, "You don't have to feel confident to be confident." I began having fun with this, taking each opportunity I could to present in front of people because I knew each time was an opportunity to sow another seed.

Here are some confidence seeds you can sow every day:

- Walk into a room with your head up confidently.
- Sit up in your chair with your shoulders back.
- Shake people's hands firmly (don't overdo it!) and look them in the eye for 3 seconds.
- Sit in the front row of events and meetings.

Act confident because God SAYS you are!

Act confident because God says you are!

Another action you can take is to go shopping and look for an outfit that exemplifies where you are headed in life. Try it on and take a picture in the dressing room. Or go the extra mile and buy it! Sow it as a seed for your future dream.

Now that we've learned about seeds of action—we're going to bring it all together in the next chapter and get started with the 21-Day Plan.

STEP 4 FUN SHEETS

What does this thought mean to you: "Too often we wait to 'feel it' before we take action"? What would show up in your life if you started to "do it now" and start before you're ready?

_____

_____

_____

Think back to how the seed-principle has been at work in your own life. Name a small action that you have you done, that has produced big positive results.

_____

_____

_____

Practice "advance decision making" for when your flesh might throw a fit. Name 3 activities you can you do to mitigate resistance when it comes.

1. _____

2. _____

3. _____

Identify the seed you'll sow in each area:

Eating: *I sow this as a seed toward my healing:*
    [   ] Bedtime eating
    [   ] This beverage _____
    [   ] Other: _____
*As an alternative, I will plan on doing this Non-Eating Activity
(walking, writing letters, cleaning out a closet, etc.) instead:*

_____

Exercise: *I commit to sow this seed of activity for at least
10 minutes:*

_____

Confidence: *I commit to acting confident when* _____

_____

Pray this when you sow:
Father, I sow _____ *as a seed in faith. It's impossible with me, but thank you, it's possible with YOU to help me!
Strengthen me in Jesus' Name. Amen.*

Don't forget to sow your seeds daily—you are going to see supernatural results quickly!

THE BRAVE
BODY METHOD
21-DAY PLAN

Sometimes you just have to put on lip-gloss
and pretend to be psyched.

—MINDY KALING

I SOLATED, EACH OF THE FOUR STEPS is itself both critical and vital. However they are meant to work concurrently. You must first **Know You Are Hot,** understand your identity, and begin thinking like God thinks about you. Then you are ready to **Inflict Damage** on the darkness by speaking out containers of creative power, your words.

After renewing your mind and speaking out how God sees you, you must continue meditating on the Word and catch the exciting vision God has for you. **Seeing the God-Painting** before your eyes will enable you to keep up the enthusiasm and momentum to fulfill your goals and dreams.

Finally, in the fourth step—you should **Start Before You Are Ready,** taking quick, decisive action by faith.

While all the steps are meant to be sequential, they also have a synergistic effect where you will begin to weave in and out of them daily. They will become part of your routine, and before you know it—you'll be *amazed* at how you feel.

You'll never want to stop!

The 21-Day Plan consists of doing **all four steps each day,** consistently for a full 21 days. I encourage you to find a regular time where you can go through the *Daily Action Guide* every day, at the same place and time.

And—the most important step, have fun while you're doing them!

Just like Jacob, who held up the spotted and speckled bark and the physical nature of his calves was altered, before you know it you are going to look different, act different, and experience joy at a whole new level.

You are going to meet the real *you*—and love it.

I love what Dr. Yonggi Cho wrote, "There are over 8,000

promises in the Bible and each is like a spotted and speckled tree for you … These promises, however, are a bit different, for these promises are all spotted and speckled by the blood of Jesus Christ."[66]

Jesus paid the price for your freedom and wholeness so that you could finally become—brave.

You can do this!

21-Day
Daily Action Guide

"K" — KNOW YOU'RE HOT

Choose one Hot Thought (from page 46) and commit to think about it for 2 minutes each day.

_____

_____

"I" — INFLICT DAMAGE

Speak one Scripture (from the list on page 92) every day. (You may want to speak more than one scripture, but commit to speak at least one!)

_____

_____

"S" — SEE THE GOD PAINTING

Practice meditating for a few minutes upon your God painting each day.

_____

_____

"S" — START BEFORE YOU'RE READY

Identify the seed you'll sow in each area:

Eating: *I sow this as a seed toward my healing:*

    [   ] Bedtime eating

    [   ] This beverage _____

    [   ] Other: _____

As an alternative, I will plan on doing this Non-Eating Activity (walking, writing letters, cleaning out a closet, etc.) instead:

_____

Exercise: *I commit to sow this seed of activity for at least 10 minutes:* _____

_____

Confidence: *I commit to acting confident when* _____

_____

Pray this when you sow:

Father, I sow _____ as a seed in faith. It's impossible with me, but thank you, it's possible with YOU to help me! Strengthen me in Jesus' Name. Amen.

Don't forget to sow your seeds daily—you are going to see supernatural results quickly!

Coming Soon

OVERCOMING EMOTIONAL EXHAUSTION

The 21-Day Plan To De-Stress Your Life,
Recover Joy & Beat Depression

A Simple Self-Care Guide for the Rest of Us

*"Here is Edward Bear, coming downstairs now, bump, bump
on the back of his head behind Christopher Robin. It is, as far
as he knows, the only way of coming downstairs, but sometimes
he feels there really is another way, if only he could stop
bumping for a moment and think about it."*

—A. A. Milne, *Winnie the Pooh*

I'M NORMALLY VERY NURTURING when people fall ill.
But when my boyfriend, Harrison got the flu, I felt
annoyed.

"Bring me chicken soup?" he whispered, in a feigned
adolescent, almost boyish voice.

You see, I'm not really that kind of girl. I *might* be able to
bring you Starbucks if you fall ill, but it's probably not going
to help your symptoms.

I told him to call his Mom if he wanted soup, I had things to do. While he moaned about seeing a bright light, and whom he wanted to bequeath his belongings to ...

I was checking email.

See, I was looking at buying my own condo at the time and was trying to stay in touch with my Realtor. A new condo had just hit the market with granite countertops, French doors and new chrome bath hardware.

I was salivating at the prospect of moving out of my current apartment with my three roommates and having my own space. This was it! I was spreading my wings, going to launch out on my own, be my own captain, and live every single-woman's dream.

At that moment, the Realtor rang to say we could draft an offer, if we moved now the seller would review it today ... and did I want to walk through it one more time?

"Wait ... you're making an offer on a condo?" Harrison began sitting up, his voice normalizing.

"Like *today?*"

Suddenly, as if he had downed a Venti Coffee, 5-Hour Energy, and an over-sized adrenaline needle had been administered to his sternum—he literally bolted out of bed, remarking:

"Lets GO! This is going to be *awesome!*"

Wait, what?

Energy.

When it fills your body, it courses through your veins, lights you up, reinvigorates your senses, and overrides any ill feelings. Energy is the lightning rod that can literally spring us into alive, awakened action. And even—raise up things we had once left for dead.

Even Harrison, laying on his sick bed, became quickened at just the *idea* of an enterprising project, a new adventure. His energy inspired me, and subsequently caused me to submit that offer—and go home that day, a proud new owner of my dream.

Friend, energy is electric, contagious, and I believe—your destiny.

I'm convinced God's will is to fill you with energy. To awaken you to new life, fill you with fresh fire, and cause you to step out of your own 'natural' energy so you can step into His!

His energy is the antidote to our own, collective exhaustion, and obtaining it isn't as elusive as we have been led to believe. This book is intended to unveil the specific strategies that we might once again, posture ourselves to receive the strength of heaven—the force of life, the energy of God.

THE FORCE OF LIFE

In ancient Latin, energy was known as *vis viva*—the force of life. Regarded as the "fire within" by the ancient Greeks, energy was translated *en-ergon,* "the source of activity."[1]

The most widely cited etymological origin of "energy," however, comes from Greek philosopher Aristotle. In his circa 350 BC *Metaphysics,* he used the term enérgeia and defined it as "having to do with that which has the ability to bring about something else."[2]

Of particular note, Aristotle desired to clarify "activity" *(enérgeia)* from potentiality *(dýnamis)* for the reason that he believed energy was "the ceaseless transformation of the potential into the actual."

For centuries, energy has been regarded as the "secret sauce" that gets things done. It is what we crave, yearn for and endeavor to gain more of. Yet, far too often, energy eludes us, slipping through our fingers as sand on the seashore. We simply cannot grasp it with enduring capability, we wonder:

Why are we so tired?

Why did our enthusiasm go?

Why are we unable to generate momentum?

Before we know it, apathy can settle in over us like a graying sky. It isn't noticeable at first, but the symptoms of procrastination, lethargy and frustration quickly tell us something is wrong. We become depleted, drained and exhausted. And the worst part?

We don't even know why.

THE SLOW BURN OF STRESS

Below the surface, the slow-and-steady burn of stress is leeching our reservoir of energy, enthusiasm and ability to feel pleasure. The Stress Management Society in the UK defines stress as "not having enough energy to meet the demands of life." If ever there was a time we are experiencing stress, it is now.

Chronic stress is at an all time high in America with over 77% of people reporting stress is causing physical symptoms.[3] And 1 in 5 people quantify their stress level as "extremely high." What's perhaps even more worrisome is that only 37 percent of Americans feel they're able to adequately manage their stress.[4]

The effects are rippling into our workplaces, our relationships and our homes. Spending over $300 billion this year on stress management alone, we are looking for relief, and we are looking for it fast.[5]

"America is at a critical crossroads when it comes to stress and our health," says American Psychological Association CEO Norman B. Anderson, PhD.

Knowing what to do, where to turn, who to reach out to, for help can be difficult when you're in the midst of an intensely stressful season. According to an American Psychological Association report, 33 percent of patients have never discussed managing their stress with a health care professional. For those suffering with depression, nearly two-thirds of the population never seek any form of treatment.

"I feel like my brain just isn't … working right," I remember expressing to a friend.

I wasn't sure if my symptoms warranted a good cry, a trip to a therapist, or heavy medication. I didn't know *what* I was experiencing! or how to communicate it.

Many times we hesitate to reach out to professionals, because there is often a stigma associated with health conditions that don't manifest in traditional pain. This often leads to a lack of action and seeking treatment.

I love the encouragement found in what Rick Warren told his congregation:

> *"It's amazing to me that any other organ in your body can break down and there's no shame and stigma to it. But if your brain breaks down, you're supposed to keep it a secret … If your brain doesn't work right, why should you be ashamed of that?"*[6]

I remember the intense confusion, and guilt I use to experience for feeling sad. Why couldn't I just be happier? I would berate myself for not being grateful for my amazing life. But I still couldn't shake the sense there was something deeper I was missing.

DRIFTING INTO A FOG OF DEPRESSION

I was 22 years old when slowly, beguilingly—I drifted into a fog of depression.

Like a boat lost out at sea the stormy waves of life swirled and churned all around me. In the middle of this boat, I sat unaffected, staring into the void. Not because I was at peace, but because my soul had vanished. I couldn't seem to feel. Anything.

It felt like a vague, uneasy sense about myself. It showed up as constant frustration. Unexplainable exhaustion. A low lying sense of guilt that I was NEVER doing enough.

I thought I was just a little "different" or not as "bouncy" as some of my peers. I didn't realize the root was deeper. I didn't realize I was addicted to negative self-talk.

It wasn't until I went to counseling that I first learned of the term "emotional exhaustion." The sound of the words from my counselors mouth became the foghorn that called me back to the shores of hope.

Dr. Gregory Jantz, founder of The Center for Hope says:

"Negative emotions along with sustained, excessive stress can lead to depression, which now overshadows other problems for which patients seek help at my clinic. Depression can be rooted in a number of problems, and those need to be addressed; simply taking a pill is not usually effective treatment. Anger, fear and guilt can all be underlying causes, even when the person isn't aware he's experiencing those feelings. A holistic treatment approach, which may or may not include medication, helps people overcome a bout of the debilitating illness, and learn techniques to manage it themselves."

My counselor explained there is a type of low grade depression, called *"dysthymia."* Regarded often as "low mood" or temporary sadness, the symptoms are not as strong as major depression. Due to it's chronic nature, many times it sets in and people don't even know it.

I learned that dysthymia is translated "bad state of mind" in the Greek. I remember remarking, "Yes. Yup. That's what I have. That's it," with my eye twitching (the latest symptom to have surfaced).

I didn't know what I was getting into—but I felt I was on the right track. Learning more, I discovered people who may be experiencing emotional exhaustion, or low-grade depression, feel symptoms such as:

- Poor appetite or overeating
- Insomnia or hypersomnia (excessive sleeping)
- Low energy or fatigue
- Low self-esteem
- Poor concentration or difficulty making decisions
- Feelings of hopelessness

As the days of counseling moved forward, and I learned about more about depression and emotional exhaustion, I slowly felt the anger, fear and guilt begin to unwind in my soul. I slowly began to feel something I hadn't felt in years.

Hope.

Instead of the slow burn of stress, I began to feel a new sensation—peace, joy, and renewal. The strangest phenomena of all occurred. I began to feel ...

Energy.

A PATHWAY TO HOPE

A critical step in my recovery occurred when I realized I was making a crucial, and damaging mistake in managing my stress. Want to hear it?

Trying to have "no needs."

I was trying so *much* to please others, I was losing myself—and a sense of who I was. I was giving so much without reservation, I never even thought to ask the question: *"What is it I want? What do I need?"*

I simply didn't want to bother anybody.

Often asking ourselves "what do I want?" feels selfish, and we should be giving, giving, giving all the time. For after all, isn't this truly "dying to self"[7] as the Scripture indicates?

However, in order for you to truly *give* of yourself, and it be a true act of altruism—it must be a choice. Losing yourself is not spiritual. Intentional generosity is.

In fact, Matthew 22:39 says, "You shall love your neighbor as yourself" not "*instead* of yourself."

It wasn't until I learned that Self Care was the antidote for emotional exhaustion that things started getting better for me personally. The strategy of a Self Care System began dismantling my depression, and slowly, I began the process of experiencing deep-seated joy.

Through reconnecting with oneself I discovered that "happy" actually is possible. That joy can be experienced in enduring measure. And that hope should be our default, rather than continual fatigue. I learned that while we can never be perfect, happy is possible. And it is found through balanced, Biblical self-care.

But, how does that look exactly? What do you do when you're numb and don't know where to start?

A STEP BY STEP SELF CARE SYSTEM

During my own recovery, I longed for a documented strategy to get me on the path toward wellness. I just wanted someone to break it down for me into small steps. Doable steps. Nothing overwhelming or complicated (because I knew I wouldn't do it).

Through my research I put together this simple *21 Day Challenge,* a "self-care guide for the rest of us."

Designed to guide you from frustration to freedom, the 21 Day Challenge will give you the tools you need to evaluate, assess and reconnect with yourself, based on 21 Proven Strategies that actually WORK.

For those who "know what they have to do but aren't doing it," this Challenge will give you everything you need have a healthier mind, body and life in 21 Days.

A wise person said, "You will never go broke from investing in yourself." At the end of these 21 Days you will

To subscribe to the free 21-Day Self-Care Challenge, please visit www.eileenwilder.com. *You will receive 21 short, motivational videos in your inbox!*

be stronger, feel lighter and actually achieve more—because you've taken the time to invest in your most precious asset: *you!*

It took years to figure out that underlying my chronic stress, my secret depression, was the neglect of my self-care. I want you to recover the energy that pulsates through your entire being, adding life, enthusiasm and bringing contagious joy—faster than I did.

As I assembled the most important steps, I was reinforced in these three critical truths I want to share with you:

1. Self Care Is Spiritual

Understand that Self Care is spiritual. Jesus was the king of self-care. He did this by taking time for himself, drawing away and nourishing his soul. In fact, it is recorded Jesus did this over 14 times in the New Testament.

2. Self Care Is Restorative

I heard this quote the other day, "Your elevation may require your isolation." Sometimes, being alone with ourselves to assess, reevaluate and reconnect is JUST the element we are missing to elevate our entire life.

3. Self Care Is Vital

If you don't take care of you, who will? Not even your spouse can carve out this time for you. You must prioritize what your spirit, soul and body need—and THEN you will be a better caregiver to the others in your world.

You are the only one who can do you.

Only you can be a mother to your children, a wife to your husband.

Only you can be that friend, and valued team-member.

Only you can bring the unique contribution you have to the world.

And we need what you have!

What would it look like if, through proper self-care, you could evaluate your mental state, and ensure you are doing the work that matters most?

What if you found a routine that re-invigorated and re-energized you, and you visited it regularly?

What if you could be elevated from a "bad state of mind" to one that's life-giving and peaceful?

HAPPY IS POSSIBLE

I remember the first time I started feeling happy again. I was sitting on my couch, reading. A calm sensation of peace and contentment started bubbling up.

Happy felt so foreign, but I loved it. I remember feeling like I had a plan, I was in control and it was all going to be okay.

Friend, as you read this, perhaps you can relate to the sense of having lost yourself. Or like me, are experiencing an unexplainable season of low-energy and fatigue. Perhaps you can resonate with a feeling of numbness, apathy or indifference in some areas of your heart.

Perhaps for whatever reason, you just feel stuck. If this is you, I want you to know you are not alone. It's all going to be okay, and your path to hope and brighter days are now unfolding before you.

A wonderful promise exists in the Scripture for those experiencing emotional exhaustion:

> *"ARISE [from the depression and prostration in which circumstances have kept you—rise to a new life]! Shine (be radiant with the glory of the Lord), for your light has come, and the glory of the Lord has risen upon you!"*
> —*Isaiah 60:1*

The Hebrew word for shine here is "owr" and its definitions include "to be or become light," "to be luminous," "to give, show light" and "to be set on fire." What this is saying is, God is a master at taking depression and turning it into brightness, to light—and even replacing it with newfound energy.

It's not only going to be *okay* for you, but as the dawning of the sun, His strength is going to reinvigorate you to such a place that your light will in turn bless others. In the days to come you are going to arise to new purpose, new plans and new strength. And even perhaps, when you think it's all over and are bequeathing your belongings …

You are going to shoot out of bed, proclaiming "this is going to be awesome!" Filled with energy, alive and fully awake.

This is going to be an incredible 21 Days, and I'm honored to journey with you. Our first step on the path? We must say goodbye to the neglect of ourselves, and once-and-for-all break our addiction to overwhelm.

Let us reclaim our birthright to live whole, well and free once again. Let us begin.

1. Feekes, Gerrit B. (1986). The Hierarchy of Energy Systems: from Atom to Society (pg. 1). Pergamon Press.

2. Lindsay, Robert B. (1975). Energy: Historical Development of the Concept (Aristotle, 17+ pgs). Dowden, Hutchinson & Ross.

3. www.stress.org/daily-life/

4. www.forbes.com/sites/robertpearl/2014/10/09/stress-in-america-the-causes-and-costs/

5. www.stress.org/workplace-stress/

6. www.christianitytoday.com/gleanings/2013/july/rick-warren-first-sermon-since-suicide-mental-health-pledge.html

7. Matthew 16:25

End Notes

1. Shaun Dreisbach, "Shocking Body-Image News: 97% of Women Will Be Cruel To Their Bodies Today," Glamour, November 17, 2011, http://www.glamour.com/health-fitness/2011/02/shocking-body-image-news-97-percent-of-women-will-be-cruel-to-their-bodies-today.

2. Ephesians 2:10 NLT.

3. 2 Peter 1:3 NRSV.

4. Adam Clarke, Adam Clarke's Commentary, Electronic Database, 1996, Biblesoft.

5. Hebrews 3:12 KJV.

6. Ephesians 3:19 AMP.

7. Ephesians 4:7 MSG.

8. Stephen Covey, 7 Habits of Highly Successful People (NY: NY, Free Press, 1989), 99.

9. Dr. Caroline Leaf, Who Switched Off My Brain (USA: Inprov, Ltd., 2009), 5.

10. Ibid., 19.

11. N.T. Wright, "Jerusalem in the New Testament," in Jerusalem Past and Present and the Purposes of God, 2nd edn., ed. P.W.L. Walker (Grand Rapids, MI: Baker, 1994), 53–77.

12. C. West, Theology of the Body Explained (Leominster, UK: Gracewing, 2003), 7.

13. Leviticus Rabba 34:4.

14. Proverbs 11:17 AKJV.

15. Ephesians 5:29 ESV.

16. Rick Albath, "Rick Albath, Security Guard Reflects On What He Lost One Fateful Night" (presentation on StoryCorps, National Public Radio, March 13, 2015), http://www.npr.org/2015/03/13/392567024/former-security-guard-reflects-on-what-he-lost-one-fateful-night.

17. John 10:10.

18. 2 Corinthians 10:4-5.

19. Galatians 2:21 NASB.

20. Psalm 10:4 NIV.

21. Luke 18:27 KJV.

22. 2 Corinthians 10:5 NRSV.

23. Ephesians 6:14-17 MSG.

24. 2 Timothy 1:7 NKJV.

25. 1 John 4:18 ESV.

26. Dr. Andrew Newberg and Mark Robert Waldman, Words Can Change Your Brain (NY, NY: Hudson Street Press, 2012), 24.

27. A. R. Hariri, A. Tessitore, V.S. Mattay, F. Fera, and D.R. Weinberger. "The Amygdala Response to Emotional Stimuli: A Comparison of Faces and Scenes," Neuroimage 17, no. 1 (2002, September 17): 317–23.

28. Genesis 1:3-29 NIV.

29. Romans 4:17 AMP.

30. Genesis 1:26-27 NIV.

31. "Soul in the Bible," Wikipedia, accessed on March 24, 2015, http://en.m.wikipedia.org/wiki/Soul_in_the_Bible.

32. Mark 11:23 AMP.

33. Mark 11:23 WEB, emphasis added.

34. Romans 10:10 AMP, brackets added.

35. Luke 4:4 ESV.

36. James 4:7 MSG.

37. Joel Osteen. Your Best Life Now. NY, NY: FaithWords, 2004.

38. Proverbs 4:21 NIV.

39. Dr. Pauline Wallin, "On Your Mind: The Mental Side of Athletic Performance," Penn Live, June 7, 2012, http://www.pennlive.com/body-andmind/index.ssf/2012/06/the_mental_side_of_physical_pe.html.

40. P. Williams and J. Denney, How to Be Like Walt: Capturing the Disney Magic Every Day of Your Life (Deerfield Beach, FL: Health Communications, Inc., 2004), 84.

41. Genesis 15:5 ISV.

42. Psalm 1:2 NIV.

43. Rick Warren, The Purpose Driven Life (Grand Rapids, MI: Zondervan, 2002), 190.

44. Ibid.

45. John 5:19 NIV.

46. The Hebrew verb "meditate on" (hagah be) includes the connotations "imagine" and "devise (in the mind)," according to a standard Hebrew lexicon, F. Brown, S. R. Driver, and C. A. Briggs, A Hebrew and English Lexicon of the Old Testament Hebrew and English Lexicon of the Old Testament (Oxford: Clarendon Press, 1951), 211, right column sub hagah.

47. Dr. David Yonggi Cho. The Fourth Dimension. Alachua, FL: Bridge-Logos, 1979.

48. "Lose Weight Your Way," ConsumerReports.org, February 2013, http://www.consumerreports.org/cro/magazine/2013/02/lose-weight-your-way/index.htm.

49. R. J. Davidson and A. Lutz, "Buddha's Brain: Neuroplasticity and Meditation," IEEE Signal Processing Magazine, 25, no. 1 (2008): 176–174.

50. Hebrews 11:1 KJV.

51. Corinthians 3:17, 18, 4:16-18.

52. Habakkuk 2:2 ESV.

53. Mark 11:24 VER.

54. Exercise is adapted from Cameron Herold's Vivid Vision exercise.

55. Joshua 1:9.

56. Psalm 37:11.

57. 2 Timothy 1:7.

58. Romans 8:31.

59. Jes Kast-Keat, Jewish Spirituality: A Brief Introduction for Christians Rabbi Lawrence Kushner (Woodstock, VT: Jewish Lights Publishing, 2001), 56.

60. Tim Ferriss, The 4-Hour Body (NY, NY: Crown Archetype, 2010), 19.

61. Helps Ministries, Inc. HELPS Word-Studies, 2011.

62. Mark 5:27.

63. Revelation 12:13.

64. Mark 5:27-28 ESV.

65. 1 Chronicles 21:24 NLT.

66. Cho, The Fourth Dimension, 39.

ABOUT THE AUTHOR

Eileen Wilder is a writer and pastor on team at Capital City Church in Washington, D.C. Like many, Eileen was plagued with the "triple threat" of anxiety, depression, and eating disorders for years.

Now she inspires women through her writing and speaking to become fierce with fear and pursue their dreams. She, her husband, and their three children live just outside D.C. in Maryland.

Read more at:
- www.eileenwilder.com
- Instagram & Twitter: @eileenwild
- Facebook: Eileen Audrey Wilder